SIMPLE PRIESTHOOD

SEAN CONNOLLY

SIMPLE PRIESTHOOD

ST PAULS

Cover image: *Last Supper* by Angelo Gherardi
Demetz Art Studio, Ortisei, Italy

ST PAULS Publishing
187 Battersea Bridge Road, London SW11 3AS, UK

Copyright © ST PAULS 2001

ISBN 085439 616 0

ST PAULS, Alba House
2187 Victory Boulevard, Staten Island, NY 10314, USA

ISBN 0-8189-0884-X

Set by TuKan, Fareham, Hampshire, UK
Printed by Interprint Ltd, Marsa, Malta

ST PAULS is an activity of the priests and brothers
of the Society of St Paul who proclaim the Gospel
through the media of social communication

for Michael and Niamh

Permission has been kindly granted to the author to reprint excerpts from the following publications:

DANIEL-ROPS, H., *History of the Church of Christ*, Volume 2: *The Church in the Dark Ages*, (translated by A. Butler et al), J. M. Dent & Sons Ltd., London. © 1959.

DE SAINT-EXUPERY, A., *The Little Prince*, (trans. Katherine Woods), first published in Great Britain in 1945 by William Heinemann Ltd., © 1991 in United Kingdom by Egmont Children's Books Ltd., and copyright in USA held by Harcourt Inc., 6277 Sea Harbour Drive, Orlando, FL32887. Used with permission.

FLANNERY, A., (ed.), *Vatican II. The Conciliar and post-conciliar documents*, published in the United Kingdom by Fowler Wright Books Ltd., Leominster, Herefordshire HR6 8DE, 1988 revised edition ©1987 by H. Costello and Austin Flannery, O.P. Used with permission of Dominican Publications, Dublin, Republic of Ireland.

HASTINGS, A., review of *Whatever Happened to Vatican II*, by Michael Winter, published in *New Blackfriars*, Blackfriars, 25 George Square, Edinburgh, EH8 9LD. © 1986.

JOHN PAUL II, *Christifideles Laici*, published in the United Kingdom by Catholic Truth Society, 40-46 Harleyford Road, London, SE11 5AY. ©1988. Used with permission.

JOHN PAUL II, *Pastores Dabo Vobis*, published in the United Kingdom by Catholic Truth Society, 40-46 Harleyford Road, London, SE11 5AY. © 1992. Used with permission.

JUNGMANN, J., *The Early Liturgy to the time of Gregory the Great*, published by Darton, Longman and Todd Ltd., 1 Spencer Court, 140-142 Wandsworth High Street, London SW18 4JJ. © 1960. Used with permission.

KENT, B., article written in *Renew*, summer edition, 1997. © 1997.

RAMSEY, M., *The Christian Priest Today*, 1987 revised edition, published by SPCK, Holy Trinity Church, Marylebone Road, London NW1 4DU. © 1972, 1985.

REPLAND, L., (ed.), *Abbe Pierre Speaks*, (trans. C. Hastings & G. Lamb), published by Sheed & Ward Ltd., 14 Coopers Row, London EC3N 2BH. © 1957.

ACKNOWLEDGEMENTS

I would like to express my gratitude to the people of St Mary's parish in Great Yarmouth and their parish priest, Gordon Williams, for the patient support they have shown me during the writing of this book. I would like to thank, too, each of the contributors for their collaboration and professional co-operation. Finally a special word of acknowledgement to John Udris for his advice and encouragement.

ABBREVIATIONS

CL	*Christifideles Laici*
LG	*Lumen Gentium*
NIN	*Novo Incipiente Nostro*
PDV	*Pastores Dabo Vobis*
PO	*Presbyterorum Ordinis*
SC	*Sacrosanctum Concilium*

CONTENTS

FOREWORD

Priesthood seems to have been in crisis ever since Vatican II with thousands of departures and a drying up of vocations. There have been numerous books by theologians which try to interpret this situation and then offer new models for priesthood which may be more viable. Rarely does a group of priests who are fully involved in pastoral work draw on their experience to speak about priesthood and then write it down. In the first part of *Simple Priesthood* Sean Connolly, a young priest of the diocese of East Anglia, offers a vivid and often startlingly frank account of what the first five years of his parish ministry were like. He works out a theology of priesthood as he goes along but it is better for being rooted in this pastoral experience. His discussion of vocation, prayer, the demands made upon him both by the parish and the life of celibacy, together with several other topics, make for lively and often humorous reading but it also offers a useful insight to lay people and his fellow priests into how one articulate priest sees his calling today. It may well deter faint hearts who are thinking about priesthood but it should also inspire others who want a real challenge. The second part of the book consists of four very personal accounts of priesthood by men who have considerable experience since they are immersed in a wide range of pastoral work. They complement nicely the younger priest's approach. I have found these different chapters an engaging and profitable read and I hope that many others in the Church will benefit from them. Priests who may feel rather isolated in their parishes should be stimulated and helped by the ideas and reflections of confreres who are doing the same sort of work. Lay people who find the lives of priests rather distant will be enabled to have a close encounter with the reality of priesthood today. The Church needs such practical and theological reflections grounded in pastoral experience if it is going to work out an understanding of priesthood which is both convincing and attractive to those who are called to follow Christ in this way.

David Sanders OP

Part One

Reality Bites

Vocation

Relationship

Prayer and Praise

Demands and Expectations

Institutions and Structures

Celibacy and Sexuality

Caricatures

Simplicity

Part One

REALITY BITES

IT WAS my first Sunday afternoon in the parish and I was quite tired to be honest. I'd only moved in on the Friday and my life was still lying in boxes in my bedroom upstairs. I'd had a pretty heavy Mass schedule that morning and suddenly I found myself answering the front door to a young lad in tears and tattered clothes, clearly drugged out of his mind, threatening to kill himself. Talk about a steep learning curve – I was in a state of shock. I suppose there is no way that seminary can prepare you for things like that. There is no way priestly training can anticipate every possible pastoral situation. The step from seminary to pastoral ministry is always going to be a large one: reality bites. Starting out as a pastoral priest has any number of hurdles. Some we manoeuvre quite successfully, others with less agility than perhaps we had hoped, and still others we just run straight into – often with quite a painful crash. Reflecting back over the past five years I cringe at some of the mistakes I have made and the situations I have allowed myself to get caught up in. But I'm still aware that the learning curve is on the incline. However much I might think I've got ministry wrapped up there's always a new challenge, a new situation, and a new mistake to be made: that's the nature of the beast, I suppose.

When I arrived in Yarmouth in 1995 both myself and the parish priest started together. We had been asked to replace a friary of four Augustinians, whose order had handed the parish back to the diocese after twenty-something years. The first hurdle, then, was not only to cope with the work that had been done by four men and now was to be done by just two of us, but also to follow four popular men. The people of the parish were understandably going through a bereavement period – they felt they had lost their community, their continuity, their priests. In place of them came two diocesans: a middle aged guy and a fresh faced first appointment. No wonder they were disappointed. For two years we had to put up with comments such as, "Well, the friars used to…" or "Fr X always…" or even (and I swear this comment was made) "The Augustinians – now they were real priests." I remember my first children's Mass one Sunday morning. It went okay and I was pretty relieved to have got it over and done with when someone said to me as they left the Church, "Yes, not bad; almost as good as Fr X. You'll do, I suppose." I thought to myself: "Well, thanks very much," but I smiled and took it as the compliment it was most surely meant. We also received one or two anonymous letters and neurotic phone calls along the lines of, "Since the friars left, all the love has gone out of the parish" and "There used to be a buzz around here until you two came." Looking back I can laugh at such nonsense but, when you are genuinely trying to do your best, such sentiments – however objectively ridiculous – still get to you sometimes. The best advice I received was from the vicar-general. "It'll be hard at first. It always is, following good priests," he'd said. "Simply nod, and smile, and bite your tongue. Sooner or later you'll become the one who has married their daughter, and baptised their grandchildren, and buried their father; you'll be the priest they know and love." It was good advice, too, because five years later on it is exactly what has happened.

Another hurdle in starting out is the whole business of settling into presbytery life and learning to live with another priest. Just the move is stressful enough. When I was in seminary I promised myself that, wherever I went, I would only take one car load of possessions with me as a sign of my simplicity. It took me two car loads to get to Yarmouth in the end and God help me when I next move; my life isn't quite as simple as I'd thought. There is something horrible about having your life boxed away, even if only for a few days. Coming into an empty and unfamiliar house is always slightly depressing too. Rooms seem dingier than they actually are: the walls stark and bare, save for the grimy marks where pictures once hung. There is that sense of absence – of course, because the room or house is un-occupied – until you yourself begin the process of making it home. Add to that stress the immediate pressure of pastoral ministry – the fact that there is little or no time to settle in properly – and no wonder new priests always seem a little fazed and distracted when they start. For the newly or-dained (or the new to pastoral ministry, as in my case I had been ordained a year already) the anxiety is threefold: new job, new house, new area (and so, to start, probably no friends). I was lucky with my first parish priest. We had met a few times before when I was a student on a placement nearby his last parish. We had a similar outlook on pastoral ministry and a fairly similar sense of humour. Fortunately we hit it off personally pretty quickly. Perhaps starting a new parish together at the same time made a difference, too, since the atmosphere between us always remained collabo-rative with a sense of joint enterprise. Whatever the rea-sons, we worked well together and even now – despite him having moved on to another project – remain good friends. Nevertheless, living and working together so closely can be hard at times, particularly in the early days when you're still feeling your way. Breakfast times are usually a sensitive point. Do you eat together or not? Do you talk or read the paper silently? Do you help yourself to a cup of tea from the pot that he has made, or make yourself a fresh brew? Silly little things, minor distractions, but they can become blown up out of all proportion if you get them wrong. It's all about learning one another's routines and respecting them as best you can. My parish priest eventually complained that I always seemed to slam my bedroom door shut at night. I was completely unaware that I did it. What made me laugh was the fact that it took him six months to build up the courage to confront me about it. I never managed to confront him about the coughing noises he made to clear his throat, however.

Another immediate hurdle is simply getting to know people and allowing them to get to know you. I recall being bombarded with names at the end of my first Sunday Mass, without a hope of remembering even one of them. I call to mind being hugged and kissed and squeezed by all ages of women who I'd never met before, as they welcomed me to the parish of St Mary's. My predecessors had obviously been of a tactile ilk and so one of the first of my many inadequacies that the people quickly came to learn was that I wasn't quite so wholesale "cuddly" as their friars. Although a lot were probably disappointed by this, I know for a fact that quite a few were more than relieved. "I never like having to kiss the priest," a parishioner told me a couple of weeks later. "Surely it depends on what he looks like," I replied. The real hurdle isn't so much people's names – these come in time, of course – but rather their characters: learning one another's ways. There is the demand or expectation of the priest to be merely the previous guy in another body: a sort of reincarnation with essentially the same character and foibles. What parishioners have to learn is that they now have a new man with new gifts and new weaknesses; not only someone with more (or less) hair, who is shorter (or taller), or thinner (or fatter), but someone with perhaps a different approach, with maybe a different style, with undoubtedly a different sense of humour. For the new priest (and I can only speak as one starting out in their first parish) the lesson to be learnt is that people are different, and not textbook examples; that people are difficult, and not always deliberately so; that people are people. One of the most startling things I discovered after priestly ordination was how seriously the laity now took me. I was twenty-seven when I first came to Yarmouth and had spent the past seven years in various institutions studying theology. Suddenly I found myself being asked for advice on bringing up children, family planning, marital problems, mental illness, teenage delinquency, coping with bereavement, Mass times in outer Mongolia (well, perhaps I exaggerate), medical problems (I definitely do not exaggerate), drug addiction, social security benefits, housing problems, local schools, and even the best chip shop in town. I discovered that off-the-cuff comments, usually intended humorously, did the rounds and more often than not found their way back to me having transmogrified through their migration into something altogether more serious. I suppose the real shock was that, for all the pastoral theology of the seminary, the clerical pedestal really does still exist and it can be rather nice at times to be standing on it (although at other times rather frustrating). Sometimes I feel the way Catholics turn to their priests is ridiculous – a sign that the laity have yet to realise fully their own vocations as people baptised into the priesthood of Christ. What do I know about bringing up children? Or, at least, what did I know five years ago when I started in the parish? What do I know about drug addiction, or mental illness, or teenage delinquency, or DSS grants? The answer is more than I did, but I had to learn pretty quickly. The real question is why should I know about these things? Is it really the priest's job to be the expert in every conceivable situation? Am I merely a modern day witch doctor? However, sometimes (and, thankfully, most of the time) I recognise these queries for what they are: the involvement of the Church, of the faith-community, in the intimate lives of her members. And since I have chosen to take up the call to be a public representative of that community, is it unreasonable to be asked to be involved in their lives? When a parishioner comes to me with a medical problem – bizarre as it may seem – what they are really looking for is not medical advice but for someone to accompany them through whatever medicine is about to throw at them. When someone asks me about their daughter's truancy it is because they need support, rather than the actual truant. And when I remember this I realise that I am not a witch doctor at all, but am someone caught up in the pastoral life of the community. The danger, though, is still that pedestal: to think I do have the answer, or might have; to think I am the answer, or might be. Even quite recently I found myself caught up in a difficult situation involving three families and their teenage children. At one point everyone involved (including the youngsters) were looking to me for the next move. My parish priest showed me the way. "You're in the middle and you shouldn't be. Whatever it takes, get out of their lives as soon as you can." I had thought I was the answer and, unwittingly, had become merely another part of the problem.

One of the most noticeable differences between newly ordained priests and their more senior counterparts is the level of idealism. To an outsider, sometimes, the curate and the parish priest may appear to be like the idealist and the cynic. This is a little too simplistic, of course, but there is a difference. Five years into pastoral ministry I can look back and see a younger version of myself with more energy and ideals, but with less experience and wisdom. There is a real danger in the early years of burning yourself out. I suppose in later years there is the real danger of being simply burnt out. I am at a stage, in my early thirties, with my ideals still but now with much of my initial enthusiasm worn away. I look to some of the older guys and see them tired and played-out. Is that what will happen to me, I wonder? What kept them going? What has finished them off? What will keep me going? What will finish me off? Will I shift at some point (or have I already begun to make the move) from idealist to cynic, from enthusiast to hack? An old school friend of mine, who has recently got married, was telling me about how his marriage – and now the hope of starting a family – had helped him to refocus his ambitions. He was no longer so bothered about his career and the likelihood of being stuck in the same job for the rest of his life. "But what about you?" he asked me. "How will you feel when you're a parish priest and that's it for the rest of your time?" The answer is that I have no idea; but I recognise that the problems of mid-life crises and lack of enthusiasm are just as likely to hit me as anyone else.

One of the roles, it seems, of the parish priest with a new curate is to pass on some of his worldly wisdom without passing on too much of his world-weariness. It's a difficult task. How to guide his eagerness without patronising him, or telling him how to do his job, or restricting him to your own limited model of priesthood. How to temper his excess without dampening altogether his ideals. Sadly, in many situations, no such guidance is given and the new priest is simply ignored and left to learn by himself. That is quite different from an honest approach where the pastor simply admits he doesn't know what to do either: this can be quite humbling and an opening to true collaboration, as both priests try to feel their way forward. The simple truth is that we don't have all the answers – either for our parishioners, or for one another, or for the future. Maybe we need to admit that a little more often, at least to ourselves.

Reflecting back upon the early days of my pastoral ministry, I recognise there were four main areas where I had to learn the job almost from scratch: hearing confessions, confronting death, school ministry, and spotting dangerous situations. There were probably many more but these four always stick in my mind. I can remember my first confession vividly. I sat behind a makeshift screen, almost shaking with nerves, gearing myself up for what was about to be said to me. I was rehearsing the words of absolution in my mind when the first penitent came in. What shocked me, what threw me – almost to the extent of making me speechless – was the simplicity of the confession: no major sins, no searching for God after thirty years away from the sacraments, no need for advice; just a humble soul once again seeking the gift of reconciliation. I realised what a total waste of time our confession practice in the seminary had been. Supposedly practical, making use of role-play, it had all centred on spotting the reserved sin, or coping with scruples, or advising other priests. Nothing about simple venial lists. Nothing about guiding an adult's first confession. Nothing about children as penitents, or deaf, elderly ladies, or people who break down and cry, or suitable penances, or when not to give advice. All this had to be learnt in the confessional itself.

Similarly, although perhaps more understandably, with the care of the dying and the bereaved. At college we did courses, to be sure, on the care of the sick and on how to administer viaticum. We were warned to be careful about what we said in front of comatose patients in case they could still hear. We were told about the different stages of the grieving process. But I suppose nothing can prepare you for your first death. Five years on in the parish, and having seen a lot of people die, I may be more professional about it all but I am certainly not used to it yet. Every situation is so different that it is a learning process in itself. At the scene of death I have been blamed, thanked, and implored. And every time I have stood there, feeling helpless and inadequate.

Inadequacy was the sentiment that most characterised the start of my school chaplaincy too. For this I had had next-to-no training or preparation. On my first day in the school I stood in the staff room and was totally ignored. I went to the canteen for lunch and was totally ignored. I wandered about the playground (trying not to look quite so sad and lonely as I was feeling) and I was totally ignored. It was only on my way out, at the end of lunch break, when I could bear it no more, that an eleven year old boy called out to me, "Cheer up, Father, it can't be that bad!" At least that made me smile. In fact it wasn't that bad really. Once I had said a whole school Mass the students began to know who I was and talk to me. Once I had been properly introduced to the staff the canteen and staff room weren't quite such a nightmare. Once a chaplaincy team was set up with lay staff from other departments I had at least a few friendly faces to look out for. Nevertheless, the very nature of chaplaincy work is hard. Largely you are sowing seeds which you will never see come to harvest. Mostly you are bearing witness and giving credibility to the gospel simply through your own humanity – by being a "normal bloke" who for some reason has a profound belief in God. I think seminaries could prepare priests more for this sort of work, and maybe they do now. Assembly-giving can be taught – at least the basic do's and don'ts. Ideas on how to celebrate Mass and para-liturgies with teenagers could be shared and seminarians could be pointed in the direction of decent resources. Pastoral plans that are already practised in schools could be examined and discussed in order to show what might be possible. Schools, too, could do more. They could devise proper induction days for the new chaplain to help him find his way around and help others to know what his role is. Co-ordinators and teams drawn from across the curriculum must be the way forward. Not quite so much should be left to the individual priest's character; he's a chaplain not a guru.

The aspect of ministry that was most painfully learnt on the ground was the aspect of risk assessment. This is a posh way of saying not getting yourself hurt or falsely accused of anything. One frightening experience happened a week before my first Christmas in the parish. It was about six o'clock, and cold and dark. I had been out all day and returned to the presbytery to find a note left shoved through the letter box asking me to visit as soon as possible – it was an emergency. I grabbed my oils and stole and dashed off out back into the night. Eventually I found the place: a dingy building full of bed sits whose entrance was down a dark alleyway. I buzzed the intercom and a voice came through: "Come on up, it's the top floor." As soon as I'd reached the room I knew I'd made a mistake. There was nowhere to sit, except on the bed, and there was only a young girl, nineteen at most, obviously an addict of some sort. The "emergency" was that she believed she was possessed. A demon was in her head telling her to hurt people. She carried a blade and told me that she used to practise wielding it in front of the mirror, fantasising about cutting someone to shreds. She claimed she would stalk the streets late at night, with her knife, waiting for the demon to tell her whom to attack. As you can imagine this was pretty disturbing stuff. What really frightened me was when she started shaking and muttering to herself, as if in some sort of internal battle. "What's wrong," I asked, a little too innocently. "It's the devil," she replied. "It's telling me to hurt you." I remember starting to shake myself and thinking, "Great, I'm going to be stabbed to death and not even see Christmas." You can never know just how fast I got myself out of that seedy little bed sit and back to the presbytery. The following day she came looking for me and the parish priest had to fob her off. When I went to the local psychiatric hospital to report to her doctor what had happened, I was told in no uncertain terms that I should never have allowed myself to have been drawn into her flat. "It's not so likely she would actually do you any harm," the doctor said. "Rather, I'd be worried about the accusations she might make against you."

My first year seemed full of examples like that. More than once I found myself in our parlour with a drug addict threatening me. Fortunately, I am six foot tall, quite broad shouldered, and have always managed to bluff my way out of a fight. I laugh now when I think about the time a man in his early twenties dropped his trousers in front of me to show me his scarred leg. I had tried to persuade him not to, but he was too drunk to know what he was doing. I dread to think what someone would have thought if they'd seen him through the window. A number of times I found myself in a basement apartment (or similar) with an alcoholic woman falling all over me. The confessional is always a risk I suppose. On quite a few occasions I have encountered rather threatening young men wanting money. There's never been any trouble, and they've always gone when I've told them to, but still the situation has been more than a little tense and scary.

Nowadays, certainly, I am somewhat wiser. I am more cautious about who I let into the house. I will not open the door late at night. I am careful who I visit and where I visit. However there are still inevitable occasions of risk. My first parish priest found himself conducting a funeral service in a crematorium full of undercover, armed police. Is this Great Yarmouth or New York, I wondered when he told me about it. Again, seminaries can't anticipate every situation but a little more guidance – even from the diocese itself – would have been nice.

So far I have looked at the initial challenge of starting out in ministry. What, though, about the ongoing challenges? How do I feel five years in? The most noticeable change has been a hardening of my overall approach. I am, sad to say, much more cynical now about the people who call at the door, spinning some story or other. How many times have I heard about a mother dying in Scotland and all they need is the fare? How many more times will I hear about a baby desperate for nappies while the social have taken the family's pay-book? In Yarmouth we have so many people calling at our front door that it simply grinds me down. Almost all are in need of something, but almost always not what they say. I don't know how to help drug addicts, and alcoholics, and down and outs, and homeless families, and recently released prisoners, and battered wives, and single parent mums, and refugees, and travellers, and runaway children, and the mentally ill, and convicts on the run – yet I have encountered all of these at one time or another. I find myself hardening, too, to the demands of genuine parishioners. I will no longer allow myself to get sucked into the pitiful neuroses of certain people. I will no longer permit myself to be manipulated by one group or another. I have to keep some sort of emotional distance from even the most heart rendering problems, otherwise I would be done for, I would be sunk. Some of this hardening is necessary. I am no use to anyone if I allow myself to become an unstable wreck, pulled in all directions. But sometimes, I wonder, have I become too hard? Do I care at all anymore?

My prayer life, too, has taken a battering. Seven years of formation was spent in seminary developing a prayerful attitude and a prayer routine. Five years into pastoral ministry I realise that I have failed to translate both that attitude and the routine to the new situation. Still, I am prayerful at times. I have, thankfully, the desire to be prayerful when I'm not actually praying. But I have never much progressed past the cycle of boom and bust. What I realise, however, is the vital importance of continuing to struggle with prayer. My relationship with God is the context in which everything else I do makes sense. When I am less than prayerful, it is then that the whole pastoral scene becomes an intolerable burden. My prayer life is the life force pulsing through my pastoral veins. Give it up altogether and I will most surely die to the whole point of my priestly ministry.

Sleep patterns are the worst aspect of my life at the moment, and late nights and disrupted sleep inevitably take their toll during the day. One of my problems is that I find it hard to say "no" and so I take on too much. I am often to be found late at night photocopying sheets for the confirmation group, or writing a talk for a retreat day, or planning a series of journey in faith meetings, or catching up with correspondence, or surfing web-sites looking for something amusing to use in a homily at the next school Mass. Sometimes I think I'm busier now than when I started five years ago. As people have got to know me and to trust me their demands have grown and grown. I need to learn to switch off now and then and make time for myself. I need to get to bed early too, but this is easier said than done.

Another difficulty I find – and one of the things that affects my sleeping habits too – is stress. I don't mean purely the stress of my own life, but also the stress I'm expected to absorb from other people's lives. Sometimes I feel like a giant sponge, soaking up their difficulties and trials. The problem is that there is often nowhere to squeeze myself out and so it all just builds up and builds up. The lonely nature of celibacy doesn't help here either. Most of my friends and family work during the week with weekends off. Of course, I work weekends (as well as most of the week) and only have one day off, sometimes not even that. It is hard to get away from it all and be with other people – people who will treat me as a friend and not as a priest: people who don't know about (or certainly don't care about) that clerical pedestal on which I spend most of my life. It becomes hard to live a life outside of pastoral ministry and yet, obviously, such "time off" is essential to my health and well-being.

Another pressure, which shouldn't be underestimated, is the toll taken by our preaching. Standing up on a Sunday morning and rattling on for five minutes might look easy; it might even seem, most of the time, as if we're just making it up as we go along. Admittedly, now and again, I have winged it in that way – but only because of the overall demands of preaching that week. To take this ministry of the Word seriously means finding a lot of time for preparation and prayer. We don't, contrary to popular assumption, only work on a Sunday; we certainly don't only preach on a Sunday. Yet the way we were taught homiletics in seminary seemed to assume this. We were told to look at the Sunday readings on the preceding Monday and start to chew them over during the week, beginning to write by Friday at the latest. So what about the weekday homilies for Advent and Lent? What about the whole school Mass on the Wednesday afternoon? What about the funeral homily on the Tuesday morning? What about the primary school assemblies, the reconciliation service, the RCIA talk, the wedding at the weekend, and the three baptisms ahead? Priests have three weekends off a year – maybe a couple more if we manage a personal retreat or an authorised trip somewhere. The rest of the time we are expected to come up with something prayerful, relevant, concise, well-communicated, and fresh week-in and week-out without any let up. This too, at times, disturbs my sleep.

The question has to be asked, then: when reality bites this much, why do I do it? Why am I still a priest? Basically because, despite all that I've just said, I love what I do and who I am. I recognise that pastoral ministry tires me out and wears me down on occasions; but most of the time it makes me come alive. I realise that my prayer life is far from perfect and my relationship with God is rather rocky now and then; but parish work is where God has led me and where I will undoubtedly find him (and, indeed, have already done so many times). I am aware that I have hardened, that I am more stressed now than ever before, that I probably work too hard, and that I am often lonely and sometimes wish I wasn't celibate; but for all that, I know too that I am the happiest I have ever been in my life. Even given this, I would want to say that priesthood is so much more than what I do or how I feel. It is what I am. The next few chapters are an attempt to draw out some sort of theology to explain that sentence, to make sense of those five words; a theology rooted in the teachings of Vatican II, to be sure, but also, I hope, in my own prayer and pastoral practice.

VOCATION

"SO WHY did you become a priest?" It's the question we all hate. It is usually posed in the most inappropriate place, at the most inappropriate time, by the most inappropriate person. I've lost count of the occasions when I've been interrogated about my motives by someone I hardly know. It's akin to someone pestering a married man about his wife: "So why did you hitch up with her, then?" Even when we do feel inclined to give an answer there is the age-old problem, where to begin. My situation is even more complicated since I am a convert to Christianity. As soon as I begin to talk about my vocation to the priesthood, I get bombarded with questions as to why I became a Catholic in the first place and what I was before. People rather hope to hear about a Damascus road experience and so what I have to tell them is usually a disappointment. Like most vocations – indeed like most conversions – my story is all rather mundane and ordinary.

I suppose the first aspect to be considered in any theology of vocation is that the primary call of God is always to holiness. The Council Fathers at Vatican II made precisely this point when they said , "not everyone marches along the same path, yet all are called to sanctity" (*LG* 32). John Paul II develops these sentiments with reference to priestly vocations when he notes in *Pastores Dabo Vobis* that we priests are firstly characterised with the "common" vocation to holiness rooted in our baptism. It is this fundamental and eternal calling from God to be "holy and faultless before him in love" (Eph 1:4) which places us alongside our

Christian brothers and sisters, uniting us all as members of the *Christifideles* (*PDV* 20). In a way this was one of the first dilemmas posed to me by the diocesan vocations director when, as a young man aged nineteen, I tried my vocation. I had spent the last twenty minutes earnestly – and rather piously – informing him of my desire to serve God. I briefed him on how I wanted to grow closer to the Lord each day; on how I aimed to develop my understanding of Christ and his Church; on how I sought to have more time to pray. He listened patiently, smiled and asked, "So why do you want to be a priest?" I thought I had just told him. I began again. He interrupted: "No, I mean why can't you do all this as a layman?" What I was talking about was undoubtedly an awakening of my baptismal vocation to holiness of life. What he was trying to discern was whether or not, in that overall vocation, there could be heard the voice of God calling me to service in the presbyteral order. I never did answer his question satisfactorily, but I assume he must have recognised something in me because, within a couple of weeks, I was packed off to a selection conference for a weekend of further interviews.

The second point to be made about the idea of vocation is that it is necessarily a call to conversion. This is implicit in the first point since, of course, any movement towards holiness demands *metanoia*: that change of heart required if we are even to begin to respond to the love of God offered us in baptism. In the New Testament we see how for each of the followers of Jesus there involves a call to conversion and a new way of living. We need only think of Simon Peter in Luke's gospel. "Leave me, Lord; I am a sinful man," he protests. "Do not be afraid," replies Jesus, "from now on it is people you will be catching" (Lk 5:1-11). There is the call, too, of Levi in Mark's gospel: "Follow me," says the Lord; and Levi gets up and follows him, leaving his money and his job in order to embark upon the road of discipleship (Mk 2:14). Similarly, the meeting with Zacchaeus: "If I have cheated anybody I will pay them back four times the amount," says the wealthy and hated tax collector. "Today salvation has come to this house," pronounces the Christ (Lk 19:1-10). We can think, also, of Mary of Magdala. Traditionally she is thought to have been a prostitute, possessed at some stage – according to Luke – by seven devils (Lk 8:2). Having been converted and healed by the teaching of Christ, she becomes one of his closest and most faithful followers, and is the first disciple to witness the resurrection. Again, a clear example of how vocation necessitates conversion.

This challenge to *metanoia* is, I think, an important element in the discernment of any kind of calling within the Church. About half way through my preparation for ordination I found myself suffering from a pretty major attack of the jitters. I began to wonder if I had either the inclination or the energy to embark upon pastoral ministry. Six years in a seminary is quite a long sentence and so – with mid term blues – I found myself questioning why on earth I would want to spend the rest of my life being pushed around from parish to parish. I began to reflect on my various place-ments, which had usually been with gregarious parish priests. I felt myself – a naturally shy and quiet man – a total disaster. I asked myself what I could have in common with the rest of the presbyterium. I began to wonder if maybe I was called rather to the monastic life, or simply to be a devout layman. It struck me that my main concerns were how to develop my prayer life and how to grow in my love of God. The whole pastoral scene began to appear to me very much like a distraction. The call to conversion came to me that summer while I was working on an island owned by Cistercian monks. Nothing spectacular happened. It simply dawned on me, labouring in the tearooms, how much I liked working with people. I found the more relaxed company of my fellow students (there were about five of us staying at the time) and their views on pastoral ministry quite appeal-ing: I saw that I did have quite a lot in common with my potential brother priests. Away from the tiredness and institutional monotony of the seminary, I began again to discern the voice of God. I began to suspect that maybe I had gifts beyond my shy and soft-spoken exterior – talents which would be forced to come to the fore in the very exercise of pastoral priesthood. The penny finally dropped when, in a conversation with one of the monks, it was pointed out that God definitely wasn't calling me to some sort of comfortable, cosy existence. Perhaps, suggested the monk, he was challenging me to grow through service. Perhaps I was being invited to use and develop my gifts – and sometimes even what I considered weaknesses – for others. In that way I would be changing my heart: becoming less self-centred and increasingly more generous, compassionate, and self-giving.

This challenge to conversion is something we find in the Old Testament too. Consider the call of Moses in the book of Exodus. Firstly, Moses encounters the holiness of God, symbolised in the burning bush. "Come no nearer," says the Lord. "Take off your sandals, for the place where you are standing is holy ground" (Ex 3:5-6). It is tempting in this life to want to spend the whole of our time sandal-free on holy ground. Some people think that is what we priests do anyway. I have one or two friends who assume that monks and nuns do nothing all day but float about their monasteries and convents caught up in some kind of beatific vision. "Live in one of their communities for a week," I warn them, "and you'll soon know the meaning of challenge." With Moses, however, the encounter with the divine soon becomes a call to service. "I am sending you to Pharaoh," says the Lord, "for you to bring my people the Israelites out of Egypt" (Ex 3:10). We know, of course, that Moses had only recently fled that country and escaped the wrath of the Pharaoh, after the news of his murder of an Egyptian had leaked out. This was why he was in Midian and to be found on Mount Horeb in the first place. The call to service, then, was literally a call to conversion: a call to turn about, return to Egypt, and confront his enemy. Naturally enough, Moses comes up with all sorts of excuses: "Who shall I say sent me? And what if they don't listen to me? No, really, what if they don't believe me? But I'm no good at public speaking – isn't there any one else you'd rather send?" Unfortunately for Moses, but rather more fortunately for the enslaved people of Israel, God is ever persuasive and he finally accepts his vocation. We know how the story ends – about the trials and difficulties that Moses faced later on; but we also know the extent of his success. By accepting that sacred call to conversion, Moses was transformed from being an outcast, sheep farming nobody into the greatest figure of Jewish salvation history. So too with any vocation. We are called, through some specific way of life, to conversion. We are challenged to become someone we would never have been had we not taken up God's call.

The third general consideration to make is that all vocations are a calling from God: the initiative is undeniably his. My earliest notion of a call came when I was seventeen. I suppose it all started when my father died. I was in my final year of sixth form without a clue as to what I wanted to do in life. The sudden death of my dad quite naturally raised all sorts of questions – not least among them, what was the point of anything. It was in my sorrowful struggle to make sense of things that the initial call to priesthood came. Maybe service as a priest – a life lived for God and for others – would actually bring me some meaning. Perhaps, I dared to think, a vocation to priesthood might be the "good" I so ardently believed God would work out of the tragedy of this death and bereavement. This train of thought continued for the next couple of years, with the element of grieving diminishing and the attraction to priesthood in itself increasing. It was more of an evolutionary development than any sort of intellectual and logical progression. A number of friends have described their call to priesthood as a sort of nagging, especially in the early days of discernment. This was true of my experience too. I used to dismiss the idea as unthinkable and myself as unworthy. I would convince myself it was all just a coping mechanism to deal with the effects of my dad's death. Nevertheless, the idea of being a priest would come back to me, growing stronger and stronger each time. It also seemed that, whenever I had successfully dispelled the idea from my own mind, the subject of vocation would be raised by the minds of others. I vividly remember once spending a long time in prayer at Westminster Cathedral, agonising over the issue and eventually deciding to forget the whole business. As I was leaving the Blessed Sacrament chapel I realised Mass was underway in the main body of the church. Walking down the side aisle, on my way out, I caught a sentence from the old priest's homily: "So I urge you: at least consider the idea of becoming a priest." I felt like Jonah, unable to escape. I can also recall one day waking up with the resolution that I wasn't even going to think about vocations anymore. Within two hours of being at work someone had asked me if I'd ever wanted to be a priest. Eventually I gave in. I applied to the diocese and found myself, just before my twentieth birthday, sitting before a bishop being told I would start seminary in the autumn.

At that young age, and without any theological training, I had believed that, ultimately, if I did have a vocation to priesthood then, eventually, I would become one whether I wanted to or not. I suppose that model of vocation is all rather deterministic, bound up in peculiar view of fate. It's an attitude I still hear echoed today sometimes. People quote Jeremiah 1:4-5: "Before I formed you in the womb I knew you; before you came to birth I consecrated you" – and I imagine little babies born already vested: little "priests-to-be". I remember my first parish priest telling a captive audience at a parish meeting about how, at his own birth, his fragile, little hand had been so tightly gripped making a fist that it was affecting the blood supply. Neither the doctors nor the nurses could get him to relax. Eventually his mother coaxed and soothed the new born child until he began to unfold his fingers, and there in his palm lay a tiny silver crucifix. "It's a sign," his mother had said to the assembled medics, "that he's destined to become a priest." I remember the story because I can picture the people's faces. They were enthralled and amazed and delighted at this miraculous tale. And then my parish priest burst into laughter and said: "Nah, not really." The problem with such "vocations from the womb" is that they are just too simplistic. What of human freedom and the myriad influences that bombard us throughout our daily lives? If these "priests-to-be" will become priests no matter what, how then can we account for the shortage of vocations in the western world? Has God really chosen to block up the flow of ordinations? Or is it more accurate to assume that we in the developed world are just not choosing to respond to his call? Human freedom, according to Paul VI, is the essential ingredient in understanding all of this. There cannot be vocations, he said in his message at the fifth world day of prayer for priestly vocations back in 1968, unless there is freedom; unless they are spontaneous offerings of oneself, conscious, generous, and total. John Paul II develops this idea in his apostolic exhortation, *Pastores Dabo Vobis*. The history of every vocation, he argues, including the vocation to priesthood, is the history of an "inexpressible dialogue between God and human beings, between the love of God who calls and the freedom of individuals who respond" (*PDV* 36). In fact the Pope is critical of any approach where God's will is to be seen as "an immutable and unavoidable fate to which man has to bend and resign himself in a totally passive manner" (*PDV* 37). In other words, all vocations are the result of free, human co-operation with the gratuitous intervention of divine grace. God calls, and we must respond in freedom. John Paul does quote Jeremiah 1:4-5 himself, however; but he puts it, alongside Ephesians 1:4-5 and John 15:16, in the context of that divine initiative of any vocation: "Thus he chose us in Christ before the world was made," says the letter to the Ephesians; "You did not choose me, no I chose you," says the Lord in John's gospel. In this inexpressible dialogue it is always God who makes the first move, never us. The Pope also comments that while we mustn't minimise the gratuity of this divine call, neither must we minimise the responsibility that goes along with our freedom. He notes that the call of the rich young man in Mark's gospel is met with refusal: "He went away sad, for he was a man of great wealth" (Mk 10:22). This is an example of our freedom, argues John Paul, but sadly a negative one (*PDV* 36). So, he points out, we have certain responsibilities. We are to ensure that we are tuned into the divine dialogue in the first place – that we are listening, despite all the distractions of our modern world. We are to endeavour to respond openly and generously, not manipulating God's call for our own purpose. We are to be unsullied by contemporary anthropologies which present us as absolutely socio-historically conditioned, or totally genetically determined. We are to avoid the influence of those notions of self-autonomy and personal choice, which in reality are little more than philosophies of self-affirmation at any cost (Cf. *PDV* 37).

We are, of course, called to holiness from before the beginning of creation (Eph 1:4). For all of us that "common" vocation finds its concrete expression in some form of "specific" vocation such as priesthood, or marriage, or religious life, or whatever. There will be times when we respond generously and times when we respond less well or not at all. This is the condition of the possibility of our free will. We may, like the rich young man, go away rather sad on occasions. Whatever our free actions, however – and our real freedom, as the Pope points out, lies in our unconditional acceptance of the divine initiative – the dialogue never ends: God calls to us from eternity. It would be wrong, then, automatically to assume that someone called to priesthood "from the womb" will definitely become a priest. There are all sorts of factors that will affect his discernment and ability to respond. There is inevitably his free will. He may simply and radically say "no". Equally, it is not fair to say that a priest who has left ministry should never have been ordained – that they were never called to priesthood in the first place. It may be that, for whatever reason, they find themselves no longer able to respond to that "specific" vocation. I feel we must avoid the idea that somehow people could ultimately thwart God's plan merely because they leave the priesthood. We should move away from the notion of "spoiled priests" as if they were some sort of shop reject or factory second. Also to be dismissed is the concept that somehow someone who does not become a priest could be eternally frustrated, because he had refused his predetermined calling. As John Paul II says, "God is truly a Father who with an eternal and prevenient love calls human beings and opens up with them a marvellous and permanent dialogue" (*PDV* 37). Whatever the limitations of our human response, it is not for us to judge that ongoing and mysterious dialogue of others with God. It is incumbent upon us, however, to support – in whatever way we can – those who have had the courage to begin to respond to such a dialogue, and those who are struggling to make sense of God's call in their given situation.

The final point to be considered in a general theology of vocation is the ecclesial dimension. As John Paul II notes, "in the Church's very name, *Ecclesia*, we find its deep vocational aspect, for the Church is a "convocation", an assembly of those who have been called" (*PDV* 34). The Pope is picking up on Vatican II here, for in *Lumen Gentium* the Council commented that the eternal Father "determined to call together in a holy Church those who should believe in Christ" (*LG* 2). If the history of every Christian vocation is the history of the inexpressible dialogue between God and human beings, then perhaps we can say that the Church – as a people called forth – is indeed the sacrament of that sacred and ongoing dialogue between God and his people. In other words, a sign that both signifies and makes present not only the vocation of all peoples to salvation, but also the manner of our human response. Whereas Paul VI noted that there can be no vocation without freedom, I believe there can be no vocation without the Church. Again, as *Lumen Gentium* puts it, God willed to save us "not as individuals without any bond or link" but rather as a people who would serve him in holiness (*LG* 9). There is no option to freelance here. When God calls us – whatever our vocation – he calls us to some definite service within the Church. When we live out our divine calling,we do so as a service to the Church and not purely for our own edification. The call to holiness – whether we mean "common" or "specific" – is never entirely a private and personal matter; it is always caught up with the very definition of *Ecclesia*, for the Church itself is called to be one, holy, catholic, and apostolic. In our vocation to holiness we are called to unity, not individualism; we are called through the apostolic community, not simply directly; we are called to serve generously the universal Church, and not merely those sections or traditions with which we have most in common. Looking to the Scriptures, it is clear that the call to holiness is not about isolated dedication to the Lord. Christ calls a college of apostles who live and work together as a group, centred around himself – not twelve individuals with nothing in common. Paul's own conversion, described in Acts, is recognised and ratified by members of the local Church community, and his subsequent preaching to the gentiles is clearly undertaken within the context of an ecclesial mission. Whether we be priests, or religious – or married, or single – our vocation is above all about saying "yes" at every level of our being to the invitation made to us in baptism: to be, not only a holy man or holy woman, but also the People of God (Cf. 1 Pet. 2:9-10).

Having presented these general points in the theology of vocation, it now seems appropriate to raise some more specific issues about the nature, method, and effect of the priestly calling. Firstly, what exactly is a call to the presbyterate? The job description of any particular priest can vary enormously from one man to the next. Within the same diocese there will be priests engaged in quite general, parochial ministry but also those involved in teaching and studying. There may be opportunities for specialised areas of pastoral ministry such as hospital, school, prison, or military chaplaincies. There may be a need for youth officers, retreat directors, canon lawyers, administrators, and so on. To make matters even more complicated there isn't only diocesan priesthood to think about, there are religious priests too. When I was first applying to try my vocation I admit I did hedge my bets a bit. I contacted not only the diocese of East Anglia but also the Jesuits, the S.M.A. Fathers, and the Mill Hill Missionaries. I was amazed by the response. Within a week of writing off to the various vocations directors I found myself on the Jesuit Today mailing list, I was given an appointment to see someone within the diocese, I received a visit from an S.M.A. Father – who "just happened to be in Norfolk at the time" – and I embarked upon an exchange of correspondence with the Mill Hills which continued right into my third year of seminary. Being a little naive I felt rather flattered by all this attention, not for a moment stopping to wonder if the current vocations shortage might have had something to do with it. In the end it didn't take me long to commit myself to the diocese. I had no connections at all with any of the other groups. I had applied to the Jesuits out of a misguided sense of my own superiority and was quickly disillusioned when I saw how long their formation lasted. I had applied to the two missionary congregations mainly because I harboured a secret fantasy of being the next St Paul; I had no idea of their particular charisms, or the extensiveness of their work, or even of what being a missionary really entailed. For such religious priests – and I speak as an outsider here – I presume the call of God is to a specific charism as well as to priestly ministry; for example to a certain kind of missionary work, or to a particular style of contemplative life, or to a radical living out of the evangelical counsels. But for the diocesan – the "GP", if you like, of pastoral endeavour – the call is simply to a sacramental service at the heart of the Church. As Vatican II reminded us, the ministerial priesthood is fundamentally ordered towards the priesthood of all the baptised (*LG* 10). The holiness of the priest – the way of his perfection – lies precisely in his dedication to the service of his people (*PO* 12). There are, of course, all sorts of service within the Church. The service to be rendered in the presbyteral order is a priestly service – in other words the service of offering sacrifice and forgiving sins. As people who, through the sacrament of order, have been configured to Christ the eternal High Priest, we are called – and have the ability and the authority to fulfil such a call – to minister in the name of Christ our Head (Cf. *PO* 2). The priestly vocation, then, is a vocation to preach the gospel, to celebrate the sacraments, in particular the Mass, and to enable the people of God to realise – I should really say shepherd them towards – their own priestly dignity.

The second specific issue to be examined is the mechanism of priestly vocation – in other words, how do I know I am called? One of the great hypocrisies of seminary life, during my time in such hallowed institutions, was the outrage caused amongst students whenever a fellow seminarian was asked by the staff to leave. Cries of, "How dare they?" would echo around the cloisters. Delegations of friends would make their way up to the rector's study on a mission of mercy in a vain attempt to change his mind. For one or two days mass hysteria and public mourning would characterise the community; and then everyone would remember that they'd never really liked the bloke anyway, and that they all thought he was unsuitable too – and so life would be back to normal. These days the whole process of formation and assessment has become much less brutal than it was once. A couple of times a year students are called in for a cosy chat with the superior. Expulsion, in fact, is quite rare – it is much more likely to be a departure of ways through mutual agreement. So unlike the old days when, so I'm told, one rector of an English college abroad used to turn up at students' doors completely out of the blue. "The next boat to England," he would say, handing over a ticket, "is tomorrow morning. I'd like you to be on it." The deferment of ministries – or of minor orders as they would have been in the past – has always been a weapon in the staff's armoury of trying to get students to pull their socks up. I remember one priest of my diocese proudly telling me how – in the 1950s – he'd got caught stealing coal for his fire from the rector's scuttle. "I got held back a year for that," he said. "Mind you, in my time, all the students for our diocese ended up getting deferred. It was sort of a tradition."

In the process of trying one's vocation, the student for the priesthood submits himself – for better or worse – to the assessment of those placed in charge of his training by his bishop. At ordination the bishop will ask for their estimation and only once the candidate has been declared "worthy" will he formally be chosen for priesthood in the presbyteral order. It is only at this stage, having been called and chosen by the bishop, that the candidate can strictly say he has a vocation. What is happening in this ritual is quite important. As John Paul II points out in *Pastores Dabo Vobis*, "the truth is that the interior call of the Spirit needs to be recognised as the authentic call of the Bishop" (*PDV* 65). We are back to the ecclesial dimension of vocation. "Every priest receives his vocation from our Lord through the Church" and it is the task of the bishop "to recognise it" (*PDV* 35). There is, then, in the mechanism of vocation not only an interior dimension, but also an exterior one. The candidate for priesthood will discern, internally, the voice of the Spirit calling him to service in the Church; but that call must equally be discerned externally by the Church community itself. God calls us to service through the community. Of course, this implies that the community, then, has a duty to foster vocations and to support and accompany those who are in the process of discernment.

The third specific issue to consider is the effect of

priestly vocation. In my response to the call of God to presbyteral service what happens to me? Sadly, I have one or two friends who have already left the priesthood. One of the constant refrains I hear from talking to them is that they found themselves at a stage where they simply wanted their lives back. Although I occasionally have my bad days, generally I have been very blessed in the circumstances of my priestly ministry and have never seriously harboured any desire to leave. But sometimes, when I'm tired, or stressed out, or emotionally drained, I find myself echoing that refrain. A part of my ministry involves being chaplain to a large mixed comprehensive, twenty miles away. I love that school – and my work there – very much; but still, driving home on a Friday afternoon sometimes, the thought does cross my mind: wouldn't it be nice to have my own life again. Part of it is simply tiredness at the end of another week. The teachers – themselves exhausted too – cheerily wave me off. "Have a nice weekend," they say, oblivious to the fact that I'm probably facing four Masses, two baptisms, an hour's confession, and a myriad of pastoral problems over the next two days. Priesthood has its compensations, of course. Not least is the thought of all those teachers returning to school with that Monday morning feeling, while I get to lay in bed for a bit, and then head off to do what I like (Monday is my day off, in case you were wondering). I suppose the point I'm trying to make is that by saying "yes" to God's invitation to service the priest's life is never again entirely his own. Of course this is true of religious, who commit themselves to a certain community or to a particular way of living out the evangelical counsels. It is true of married people, whose lives get caught up in loving and caring for one another and for their children. The reality is – for all of us – that service means self-sacrifice, and we will never be entirely happy in our vocations until we accept that. "None of us lives for himself," as St Paul reminds us: "We belong to the Lord" (Rom 14:7-8). And as Jesus himself says, "the Son of Man came not to be served but to serve, and give his life as a ransom for many" (Mt 20:28). In baptism we have "put on Christ" (Gal 3:27) and are called to share in his priestly, prophetic, and kingly mission. For those of us in holy orders, however, this sharing takes on a new dimension. By being configured to Christ the Head through priestly ordination we have accepted a public role. By our service we are to proclaim the presence of Christ the servant-king in the lives of others. By our sharing in the ministerial priesthood of Christ we are to be a living sign of the meaning of sacrifice for the whole Church. By our dedication to the Word we are to underline the prophetic truth of God's promise of *Emmanuel* – that God is with us. In other words, we are to become a living sacrament: a showing forth and a making present of the true nature of the essential dignity of all who are baptised.

It is for this reason that the permanence of ordination is upheld in the Church's tradition. Christ is the Word for all eternity and can never lose his priesthood. As the letter to the Hebrews says, quoting from Psalm 110, "You are a priest forever." Since the Lord has a perpetual priesthood, "it follows then that his power to save those who come to God through him is absolute, since he lives for ever to intercede for them" (Cf. Heb 7:22-25). If we are to say that, through baptism and confirmation, we are somehow made sharers in Christ's priesthood it makes theological sense to conclude that we share, too, in it's perpetual, eternal nature. If we do not, rather than participating in the genuine article, we are merely exercising a sort of temporal, earthbound version of it. We have been called from all eternity and, once we co-operate with God's divine initiative and submit ourselves to baptism, we are forever "consecrated to be a spiritual house and a holy priesthood" (*LG* 10). Similarly, by being configured to Christ the High Priest in an essentially new way through ordination – so as to be able to "act in the person of Christ the Head" (*PO* 2) – it makes sense to understand that new configuration as again perpetual. Christ's priestly mission doesn't come and go and neither does our participation in it through the sacraments of initiation and ordination. Thus the Church speaks about an indelible stamp, or a character, being imprinted upon our souls in the sacraments of baptism, confirmation, and holy orders. What is really being said is that, through these sacraments, we are radically and ontologically changed. We are being re-created, which is the whole process and point of salvation (Cf. Rev 21:1-7).

The process of priestly laicization, then, can be somewhat misleading. The canonical manner by which an ordained minister is dispensed of his obligations and allowed to remain in good standing with the community is not the same as an annulment of his orders or a reversing of his priesthood. He is, and shall remain for all eternity, configured to Christ the High Priest. Laicization merely relieves him of his ministerial duties and removes his clerical status in the eyes of the Church. It is very much a dispensation – an exemption made for one person at one time by the community for the good of all concerned. However, with laicization a reality, this raises again the question of our human freedom.

I discussed earlier how vocations depend upon human freedom – how God's gratuitous initiative of grace needs to be met with the human *fiat*. Of course our basic free will is never overruled by God's sovereign plan for us and so we can speak about a daily need to accept our vocation. John Paul II comments that, in a sense, "one can speak of a vocation within priesthood" (*PDV* 70). What he means is that priestly ordination is not the end of our response to God's call but is, in fact, the fundamental beginning of a set of new responses. We are continually called to be ever more holy; we are ceaselessly encouraged to live out our sharing in Christ's priesthood. Nevertheless, once the divine vocation has been fundamentally accepted – through initiation or orders – a new and irrevocable covenant has been established between God and the individual in the midst of the Church. We may, as men ordained to the presbyteral order, be invited to immerse ourselves again and again into the mystery of Christ the High Priest, but we are not invited to draw ourselves up and out from this unfathomable well of grace and sanctity. However – as with all things – concupiscence and human sin play their part. In our current age of transient consumerism it is extremely hard to stand out as men and women of fidelity and commitment. The nature of our free will, the circumstances of our modern world, the structures and pressures of our working environment may all conspire to make us unable to make that daily "yes" to God. This is not something new. The books of the Old Testament record the infidelities and distractions of the people of Israel to the covenant of the Lord. Consider the book of Numbers in which, even on their journey to the Promised Land, the people rebel and are stubborn of heart and will. Read about the missions of the numerous prophets who find themselves charged with calling the people back to a renewed and revitalised living out of the *Torah*. The prevailing message, however, is always the message of *hesed*: that whatever our human infidelity, Yahweh will remain true, steadfast, faithful, and uncompromising in his love and in his covenant promise. As priests of the New Covenant – sealed with the blood of Christ – we can also hope that, however unfaithful we may be at times, God will never cease to call us to a new and more abundant life.

RELATIONSHIP

THERE is a scene in Antoine de Saint-Exupéry's story, *The Little Prince*, where the youthful traveller comes across a fox for the first time. When the prince asks the fox to play with him he is told that he must tame him first. Until that time he will be to the fox just a little boy – no different from a hundred thousand other little boys. "If you tame me," the fox says, "it will be as if the sun came to shine on my life. I shall know the sound of a step that will be different from all others." The little prince will become for the fox, then, someone "unique in all the world" because, through the process of taming, both will have embarked upon a relationship. What de Saint-Exupéry has written is, at least amongst other things, a parable about the dynamics of friendship. It is the story of a travelling prince who leaves behind his small planet and a rather vain rose which had kept him company – precisely to get away from the flower's conceited demands. "I was too young to know how to love her," the prince explains early on. Yet it is in his escape, and in his journey across the universe, that the prince comes to appreciate the true beauty of his little rose. Towards the end of his adventures he encounters a field of roses identical to his own and is almost devastated with the realisation that his flower is not unique in appearance. But, having tamed the fox, he begins to understand that what makes his rose beautiful and unique is not its appearance but his love for it. As the fox confides to him, "It is only with the heart that one can see rightly; what is essential is invisible to the eye." As the little prince tells the field of identical roses, "You are beautiful, but you are empty. One could not die for you." He concludes, "You are not at all like my rose. No one has tamed you. To be sure, an ordinary passer-by would think that my rose looked just like you. But in herself alone she is more important than all the hundreds of you other roses... because she is my rose."

This idea of relationship lies at the heart of our Christian theology of creation. If we look to the creation accounts in Genesis (either the Priestly source account in Genesis 1-2:4a or the earlier Yahwistic account in Genesis 4b-3:24) we find the provision of all sorts of levels of association and interaction. God says, "Let us make man in our own image, in the likeness of ourselves, and let them be the masters of the fish of the sea, the birds of heaven, the cattle, all the wild animals and all the creatures that creep along the ground" (Gen 1:26). From the very first moment of our existence, then, we are placed in relation to the rest of our environment – as God's stewards, or viceroys; masters representing on earth the Lordship of Yahweh over his creation. Again, in the Yahwistic account, the Lord says, "It is not right that man should be alone. I shall make him a helper," and so the wild animals are created, and the birds of heaven. Eventually, as we know, God fashions woman from Adam's side to be the perfect helpmate – "bone of my bones and flesh of my flesh" (Cf. Gen 2:18-25). Here too reciprocity, interdependence, and relational harmony are envisaged from the very first moment. However, this theme of relationship runs deeper than merely our interconnection to (and differentiation from) one another and the rest of creation. We are created in the image and likeness of God himself. We are made to reflect the Triune God – that eternal dynamic of the loving relations of Father, Son, and Holy Spirit. Our very make up, our essence, depends upon relationship. In the story of *The Little Prince* the rose is unique because it is loved by the young boy. However, if that relationship didn't exist between them, the rose would still be a rose – it simply wouldn't have the value that it does for the prince. On his travels, when he looked up into the heavens, the boy wouldn't believe that all the stars were "a-bloom with flowers." But the rose would still exist – it would still be there, on his planet, vain and demanding as ever. In our creation, however, we are not only unique because God loves us, but we exist because God loves us. Without his love we cannot be. We are creatures dependent upon our creator. We can see the disaster and disharmony caused when we deny that basic ontological reality in the sin of Adam. To eat of the tree of knowledge, to attempt to be gods and to forget God, to usurp the role of the creator and deny ourselves to be mere creatures – all of these things bring about a breakdown in our relationship with the Lord, with one another, and with the whole of creation.

With the New Covenant, with the death and resurrection of Christ, there comes about a new creation. The paradise that is lost in the book of Genesis through human sin is now transfigured and made new in Christ's victory over sin and death. As St Paul says, "the whole of creation has been groaning in labour pains" until that day when it might be "freed from its slavery to corruption and brought into the same glorious freedom as the children of God" (Cf. Rom 8:18-25). Where there is a new creation there is also a new set of relationships. In the process of salvation we are not merely restored to that creator-creature-creation harmony portrayed in Eden. We are invited to become adopted sons and daughters of God, co-heirs with Christ. Creation itself will be a "new heaven and a new earth" where there will be no sun or moon, no need for lamplight or sunlight, because God himself will shine on us (Rev 22:5). That is why theology talks about an ontological change, or an indelible stamp or a character, being placed upon our souls in baptism and confirmation. We are being remade. Our essential relationship with our God is created anew as we become his adopted children. And, if there is a radical change at the level of ontology, then our baptism and confirmation must also affect our relationships with one another and with the environment. We are brought into a new reciprocity with others as members of the one body of Christ. We are no longer the viceroys of God upon the earth made in the *imago Dei*, but rather we are now the *imago Christi* – the image of Christ, continuing his redemptive work to set free the whole of creation in the power of the Spirit.

What can be said of the ontological change in the sacraments of initiation must also be said of that essential change made through ordination. The Council Fathers at Vatican II were clear in their reception of the teaching of Trent that the sacrament of holy orders, like baptism and confirmation, confers an indelible spiritual character that cannot be repeated or conferred temporarily. As the Fathers pointed out, the ministerial priesthood may be ordered towards the common priesthood of the faithful, but it also differs "essentially and not only in degree" (*LG* 10). If the difference is, as the Council argued, at an essential level, then it means something must have happened to the priest's make up – to his ontology – when he was ordained. To my mind it makes sense to interpret this at the level of relationship since our very essence is relational. In other words, by being ordained to the presbyterate the candidate enters once again into a new and permanent relationship with God, with his people, and with the rest of creation. What this means in practical terms I shall attempt to draw out in the next three chapters, but with one proviso. The work of our salvation – which includes these ontological changes – is at root a mystery because it is caught up with the mysterious inner life of the Trinity. To discuss the exact meaning of the indelible stamp of the sacraments is beyond me. To point to specific events, and moments, and times and to say, "There, look, at last this is conclusive proof of what I'm trying to show," is rather foolish and somewhat conceited. All I can do is point in the direction of where I believe this theology of priesthood leads us. As the fox so wisely confided to the little prince, "It is only with the heart that one can see rightly; what is essential is invisible to the eye."

PRAYER AND PRAISE

AS I start to write this chapter I feel that I must, in all honesty, admit to being slightly out of sorts with my priesthood at the moment. It's February and, let's face it, February is a funny month for most of us: winter lingering on and spring not quite ready for us; short days still and cold, but brighter than they've been. A wistfulness, almost, in the air; and this year I find there's a wistfulness about my priestly ministry too. One unsettling factor (in addition to the weather), which is probably affecting me more than I care to admit, is that my immediate future is uncertain. I have been in the same parish now for five years, but in the last few months discussions have been underway for a move – not to another pastoral placement, but back into the area of academia for further studies. It's an exciting prospect in many ways but a daunting one too. I have made my home not only here in Yarmouth but also in the type of ministry I have been called upon to exercise. Soon, possibly (for nothing is as yet confirmed), and for a couple of years at least, all that will change. Of course there are other factors affecting me too, not least the inveterate challenge of celibacy. There is a certain pastoral boredom at the moment (Christmas has long since past and we're not yet into the rich and fertile pastures of Lent); and let's not forget plain and simple tiredness. The American Jesuit, John Powell, once published a collection of his writings under the title, *Through Seasons of the Heart*. Because we preach the gospel week-in and week-out, because we are entrusted with upholding the faith and the promotion of

Church teaching, because we endeavour to remain "on message" as much as we can, people often assume that we priests are constantly dedicated and single-minded in all that we do. For me, at least, I admit to a professional commitment (and even a certain zeal), but I am a long way off the true single-heartedness that becomes holiness. Like a lot of people – and like a lot of other priests, I suspect – I am still growing through the seasons of my heart. As I write this I'm unsure whether – for me – it is the first signs of spring or winter still: February is a funny time all round. There is a certain irony in being asked to write a book about priesthood and then, halfway through writing it, finding yourself rather uncertain and unsure about the whole presbyteral endeavour. It is ironic, too, that such feelings should strike as I attempt to write this particular chapter, *Prayer and Praise*, since I believe that this subject matter cuts to the core of why I'm feeling as I am.

Our primary and defining relationship lies with God. This is the essential message of the Law and the Prophets; this is at the heart of the Good News of Jesus Christ. In the book of Exodus Moses is told by the Lord, "I shall take you as my people and I shall be your God" (Ex 6:7). In the first book of the Kings the prophet Elijah challenges the people, assembled at Mount Carmel, to stop hobbling first "on one leg, then on the other" in regard to their religious affiliation. "If Yahweh is God, follow him," he argues, "if Baal, follow him." We know how the story concludes, with the massacre of the false prophets of Baal and the people's acclamation: "The Lord is God! The Lord is God!" (1 Kings 18:20-40). Ezekiel prophecies a time when the Lord "shall make a covenant of peace" with his people. "I shall make my home above them," the Lord says through his prophet, "I shall be their God, and they shall be my people" (Ezek 37:15-28). In the life and teaching of Christ we have the clearest example of the importance of our relationship with God. "The Word became flesh," reads the prologue to John's gospel, in order to give us "the power to become the children of God" (Cf.

51

Jn 1:1-18). And finally, in the book of Revelation, we have the vision of the new creation in which the holy city, the new Jerusalem, appears as "a bride dressed for her husband." A loud voice cries out: "Look, here God lives among human beings. He will make his home among them: they will be his people, and he will be their God, God-with-them" (Rev 21:1-4). The whole thrust of salvation history, then, is the movement towards that new relationship and unity with God as his adopted children, which replaces and surpasses the original paradise of creation lost through Adam's sin.

This relationship with God is something dynamic rather than static. It involves dialogue rather than monologue. It entails movement and growth rather than inertia and decay. It is a process of being drawn up into the inner life of God himself, as opposed to being simply drip-fed from on high. It is an eternity of divine initiative met by our own (usually poor and rather inadequate) human response. It is a relationship of love. When we find ourselves in love with someone else there is a strong desire to be with the other. We create in one another reasons for our love. We grow and deepen (ideally) in our friendship through communicating how we feel, through spending time together. Similarly with God. When we begin to realise that God does love us completely and radically and when, finally, we begin to respond to that love, so we are drawn up into him and created anew – we are made loveable because we are allowing God to love us. The language of our divine friendship, the communication of such unfathomable love (and the way we spend time together), is precisely the language of prayer and praise. As the Council Fathers noted at Vatican II, concerning the liturgy, "in this great work... God is perfectly glorified and men are sanctified" (*SC* 7). It is the "summit toward which the activity of the Church is directed; it is also the fount from which all her power flows" (*SC* 10). In other words, in our prayer and praise we not only express and celebrate the relationship we have with God but at the same time we allow him to deepen it.

For the ordained priest, the man who has been configured to Christ the Head, there is a shift in that fundamental relationship. The prayer and praise of a priest differs in some sense from that of the lay-faithful. I do not mean here that the priest is in any way holier, more prayerful, or "above" the baptised lay-person. I simply mean that there is a different character to his prayer in virtue of the ontological change effected through his ordination. The prayer life of a priest is never purely a private affair. He will, for sure, have times of personal prayer but even at these times he will represent the whole body of Christ; even in these quiet, unofficial moments he will be bringing his people before God the Father. He has, for all time, been configured in a new way so as to participate in the mediatory and intercessory role of Christ the High Priest. The clearest example of this is, of course, in the celebration of the Mass. In the convocation of the family of the faithful, the priest stands and prays on behalf of the whole Church – uttering before God the praise of all present. This prayer of the community is made in response to the loving presence of the Lord who has already made himself felt in the midst of his people and who, through the actions of the priest and the power of the Holy Spirit, chooses to dwell with us substantially in the Eucharist.

There is an image in Michael Ramsey's book, *The Christian Priest Today*, which perhaps better sums up what I am trying to say. Ramsey noted that the original meaning of the Greek word which we translate as "intercession" was not "to make petition" or to pray or speak for, as we tend to think. Rather it was a notion of presence. It meant encountering someone on behalf of, or in relation to, others. And so Ramsey argued that the image of Christ the High Priest that we find in the letter to the Hebrews is an image of the Lord being in the presence of his Father *for us*. We read that Christ has entered the sanctuary of God once and for all

(Heb 9:12) and that he has taken his seat forever at the right hand of God (Heb 10:12) where he lives forever to intercede for us (Heb 7:25). What is presented here, according to Ramsey, is a theology of being, rather than doing. Christ is *for us*. By virtue of our ordination, we priests now are *for others*. We share in this intercessory ministry of Christ the Head. Ramsey also used the image from the Old Testament of Aaron, who entered the Holy of Holies once a year wearing a breastplate inset with twelve jewels, representing the twelve tribes of Israel. This was a ritual sign that as he approached Yahweh he had the people near to his heart (Cf. Ex 28:15-30). "Being with God with the people on your heart is the meaning of the divine office, of the Eucharist, and of every part of your prayers and your service of the people," said Ramsey, speaking to candidates about to be ordained. Our relationship to God, then, has been changed through our ordination to the presbyteral order to become always intercessory, so that we are always standing before God for others as much as for ourselves.

I confessed at the beginning of this chapter to feeling rather out of sorts. It strikes me, even as I write, that this is because I have stopped praying. Oh, I say my prayers all right: I celebrate Mass each day, I am dutiful in my observance of the liturgy of the Hours; I even give over time to meditation – although not as much, or as often, as perhaps I should. I can write about prayer, and preach about prayer, and give retreats on prayer. I can recite the poetry of the psalms, and I can read the Word of God, and I can sit and think clever and intellectual thoughts, and sometimes – maybe sometimes – I can allow the Lord to touch my heart; but most of the time I'm not praying – or at least not in the way I'm called to pray. Even in my quietest moments, just recently, I've begun to notice that I'm not really present before God. I'm simply daydreaming, or theologising, or planning the day ahead. So far removed from that intercessory prayer of Christ himself to which I'm supposed to be configured. And it is this lack of prayer – of being prayerful

– which I now see as the major reason for feeling the way I do.

One of the great problems, I believe, which faces us as priests is that prayer is our job. "Say a prayer for me, Father," is a constant refrain we come across in pastoral ministry. So often I smile, and reassure, and then completely forget. "Could I get a Mass card signed?" is another such request, and so often I tie myself up with special intentions, and anniversary Masses, and prayers for the sick, and then get a barrage of "I didn't hear my auntie's name mentioned" complaints when occasionally I get it all in a muddle. We are called upon to preach each Sunday (and weekdays in Advent and Lent); we have to prepare the sermon for the funeral service, and the nuptial Mass, and the baptism on Sunday afternoon; we are called to give school assemblies, and radio talks, and write pieces for the local paper – and all of these are to flow from our prayer lives. We say Mass once a day (and three times on a Sunday); we lead Benediction, and we strive to say the Office; we pray before meetings, and after meetings (and, if they're boring, quite often quietly within meetings); we bless things, and we pray with people – and in the midst of all this prayerful activity we suddenly wake up to find that we're not really praying at all. We have become professionals: sacramental machines, dispensaries of the glib word, reader of prayers – but not so much pray-ers. Such professionalism, I believe, is a sad distortion of what we priests are called to be: those who celebrate the sacraments with the people, enabling them to stand before their God; those who vocalise the Word of God already present in and speaking to the hearts of their community; those who gather and shepherd their people to live lives bursting with the vibrancy of their own prayer. Prayer is seen as our job, when in fact our job is to be a sign of the prayerfulness of all the faithful. Prayer – at least at times – has been delegated by the people to the priest, when in reality it is the priest who should be helping the people to pray themselves.

Not surprisingly, then, this professionalism begins to affect our personal spiritual lives too. We can become worn down with the demands made upon us to pray. Our meditation can become purely an exercise in thinking through our next homily; our sacramental celebration just another thing to be got through, to be done. In one sense we are moving away from the model of intercessory prayer proffered by Michael Ramsey. Striving to pray for others we have ended up "praying" as an activity rather than being prayerful. We are "doing prayer" instead of exercising that new and fundamental relationship with God, which we entered upon ordination, as men who are before God for others. Furthermore, making prayer a "job" – something we do – risks making God merely an option. If prayer is our job, then our relationship with the Lord becomes simply a part of our working environment. Maybe God becomes the boss. There is the danger that when we don't feel we're at work we no longer feel we're standing before the Lord. And so we metaphorically (and sometimes literally) "go on holiday" and don't even look at the Office, or try to find time for contemplation, or want to say a Mass. We switch off, and opt out, and give up.

When we were in seminary a lot of emphasis was placed upon the seriousness of prayer. Structures were in place, such as times of morning meditation, community Mass, celebration of the Office in common, Eucharistic adoration, and so on. We found ourselves spiritual directors and we attended conference days and retreat weeks. We were daily surrounded by other living examples of the importance and power of prayer. But suddenly, as a diocesan priest working in a busy parish, all that has gone: structures, directors, retreat programmes and the like. Now no one chases you if you don't get up to pray each morning; no one asks when you last said Prayer during the Day. Some of us, it is true, manage to retain a "soul friend" of sorts, but a lot of us don't. Some of us try to fit in a decent sized retreat each year, but a lot of us can't (or won't) and merely fulfil the canonical minimum of five days every two years. Sadly, there are some of us – for all sorts of reasons – who don't even manage that. And for most of us, post-ordination, the practice of common prayer is pretty uncommon (except when we're doing our job!). The attitude of formation seems to be a bit like teaching someone to swim. Plenty of vigilant assistance at the start – orange, inflatable armbands and all – but once you've learnt, you've learnt. Even if prayer was something – like swimming – which you learnt and then got on with, that doesn't allow for the parochial equivalent of the mid-Atlantic in which so many newly ordained priests find themselves sunk. But, of course, prayer isn't fundamentally an activity, which you're either good or bad at. It is actually the expression of our relationship with God – it is the language of an ongoing and deepening friendship with the Lord. And for the priest, it is an expression of his new identity as one who intercedes; one who stands before God with his people on his heart. It is no wonder, then, that priests in trouble are more often than not priests who have given up on prayer.

There are some diocesan structures in place to support us in our prayer lives, but these depend very much on the area in which we minister. There is the Jesus Caritas fraternity, and may be other similar forms of ministry to priests. Some dioceses offer annual retreats. Almost all have study days – although these are usually on subjects such as tax returns and covenants and rarely on prayer and praise. But, whatever the actual provision, the biggest hurdle would seem to be a cynicism amongst the clergy themselves. Directors of ongoing formation are forever pulling their hair out as to why priests tend not to turn up in any great number at whatever is laid on for them. In my opinion it comes back down to our professionalism. We know how to pray (whether we do it is another thing altogether) and so what else can possibly be on offer? We're just going to be told how to do our job – and who wants to be told that? Perhaps another contributory factor to such cynicism is that we priests tend not to talk about our prayer lives very much. For sure, we talk about prayer – but never, or rarely, do we talk about *our* prayer.

What, then, of my prayer? A big part of me would want to say that my prayer life is rubbish. And a smaller part of me would probably try to mitigate that sentiment to "rubbish at the moment." If, by this, I mean that I rattle through the Office some days (or maybe most days?), or that I can't get through even half an hour's meditation without twenty-eight minutes of distraction, or that I sit down to pray some evenings and simply fall asleep in my chair, or that I'm hopeless at keeping to rigid times and set patterns, or that I've never quite got to grips with a routine of spiritual reading: if this is what I mean then, without doubt, I can say that my prayer life is "rubbish." But it strikes me that all this is simply about what I am doing, whereas prayer – surely – is about what God is doing in me; about how he is inviting me to respond to his love. If prayer is actually the language of this relationship with the Lord, then I have no business to say that it is "rubbish" because – despite my tiredness and laziness – there is something incredibly dynamic and creative going on: God is loving me – and trying to tell me how much he loves me; and bit by bit (sometimes almost imperceptibly) I am beginning to love him back.

In the past I have tended to worry and fret about the quality of my personal prayer. Am I doing it right? Is it long enough (or too long)? Why is it so boring? How come sometimes it is all boom, and at other times merely bust? Do other priests – do other people – feel as inadequate and as hopeless as I do about it all? These are silly, stupid worries on my part. Again the focus has slipped back to prayer as activity; something I do – all eyes on me, with maybe an unfavourably comparative nod in the direction of others. Again I am using a model of prayer that views it as my job and so I worry about how "good" I am at it. Yet, as all the great pray-ers of history remind us, the focus is supposed to be on God. It strikes me that in the celebration of the Church's liturgy we are not endlessly worrying about our ability. We know that what we are doing gets caught up with the prayer of the whole Church and in the prayer of Christ himself. We know that the focus of the liturgy is not ourselves but the God who saves us. Perhaps we can adopt a similar attitude to our times of personal devotion and contemplation. However "good" or "bad" I think I am at meditative prayer, I can still resolve to spend a certain amount of time each day before God with my people on my heart. I can still be aware of linking in my private prayer with that continuing intercessory prayer of Christ to whom I am configured.

One area that I feel I neglect in my personal prayer is the area of praise. Naturally, thanksgiving and praise are the hallmarks of the Church's liturgy which I celebrate each day; but in my own more private moments I find it an aspect that is sadly lacking. Possibly this is because my prayer tends toward the cerebral. I pray with my brain and with my intellect whereas sometimes, I know, I am called to pray with my heart and with my emotions. Perhaps then my response to God's gratuitous love for me would become more than merely an intellectual assent and rather an awakening of the real me: an outpouring of heartfelt praise and gratitude towards so great a God.

Another problem area, I find, is always that uneasy stand off between prayer and sin. Ingrained in my psyche is the notion that unless I am free from sin I am not really free to pray. There is a distinction to be made between sin troubling our prayer and sin destroying our prayer. It makes complete sense that those things that lie on our conscience should arise time and again in our moments of prayer – after all, sin is a reality of our lives and in praying we place that reality before God. But it is a nonsense to allow sins – however great or small – to turn us away from praying altogether. Christ himself addressed this issue: the parable of the Pharisee and the tax collector (Lk 18:9-14), the parables of the lost sheep, the lost drachma, and the prodigal son (Lk 15:1-32) all tell of God rejoicing at the return of the sinner; of God "putting at rights" the one who sins. Knowing all this, there are still certain sins that affect me to the extent that I stop my daily prayer – sins which cause a wholesale breakdown in my relationship with the Lord. There are two options it seems to me: to pray "out" of my sin – to try and listen to God calling me through my prayer to a deeper repentance. Or the alternative, which I normally follow: to try and "put at rights" my sins by myself and then return to prayer. Of course I can never put things right. I need God's saving grace and the only way of receiving it is to turn again to him with a contrite heart. A Scripture text that I find especially helpful in this regard is that of Joel 2:12-13: "But now – declares Yahweh – come back to me with all your heart, fasting, weeping, mourning. Tear your hearts and not your clothes, and come back to Yahweh your God, for he is gracious and compassionate, slow to anger, and rich in faithful love." However imperfect I might be, the call to perfection in prayer is always made to me as I am. It is made to me while I am still in my sins. It is, precisely, a call to conversion; the challenge of God's love. I wonder if, in fact, it is this challenge that puts me off prayer, rather than my actual sins themselves. Maybe I don't pray some days because I don't want to be asked to change some days; because I don't actually want to grow, I don't want to repent, I don't want to be loved. I am, on some days at least, too caught up in my self-love.

To my mind, the experience of prayer is not unlike the experience of being short-sighted and then being given a new pair of spectacles by an optician. For years I had managed to get by with poor eyesight, not really noticing that things were getting rather fuzzy and blurred around the edges. Now and then, maybe, I suspected that something wasn't quite right, but in my vanity I tried not to admit it to myself. Then, after a routine eye check and having ordered a pair of frames I put the glasses on. Suddenly everything comes into focus. At once I can see what I've been missing.

Similarly, when I have let the routine of my personal prayer slip for a while, and when I return to it again, suddenly my life comes back into focus; suddenly a balance and a perspective which was hitherto lacking (but often unnoticed) is now restored. People have commented to me how, although such personal prayer demands taking time "out" of the day, the effect always seems to be one of creating more time. This rings true for me too. The hassles, the worries, the stress of each day are given a proportionality; no longer do they consume so much of my time and energy. Through meditative, contemplative prayer the whole day becomes clearer.

The realisation, for me, that I'm not really praying at the moment explains a lot about my mood. It would seem obvious that if my relationship with the Lord is slightly out of sorts then it will have a knock-on effect upon my other relationships too. If prayer becomes mere work, then how much more so will the pastoral scene, my relationship with my brother priests, and my life of celibacy? The people I am called to intercede for will become a set of problems to be solved or avoided. Other priests, far from being members of an intimate brotherhood, will become a threat, or an irrelevance, or mere colleagues. Celibacy, supposedly a sign of my interior dedication to Christ, will become a burden – an unfair professional requirement that I either begrudgingly accept or secretly side-step.

Clearly, then, we do need to pray – pray as an activity; but in such a way that it is expressing something much more fundamental – prayer as a way of living: being prayerful. Our prayer is to be the expression of our ongoing friendship with the Lord – not simply something we do, or an obligation we fulfil. There will, of course, be times of boom and bust – days when prayer seems easy and we're relatively enthusiastic, and days when it all seems as dry as dust and we simply can't be bothered. But, if our prayer and praise is above all about the deepening of that essential and intercessory relationship with the Lord, then – I believe – these periods of bust will become gradually less disconcerting and less distracting. We will come to know and trust that God is there, loving us always; we will want to spend time with him, interceding for our people. The challenge, I suppose, will always remain for us: the challenge to avoid becoming the professional; the challenge to make prayer our life rather than simply our job.

DEMANDS AND EXPECTATIONS

"I HAVE made myself all things to all people," St Paul wrote to the Church at Corinth, "so that I might save some of them" (1 Cor 9:22). I know how he felt. In just five years of pastoral ministry I have found myself being a children's entertainer, an intellectual, a pub comedian, a critic of fine art, a football manager, a dramatist, a referee, a bouncer, a tennis coach, a computer nerd, a musical director, a bus driver, a quiz master, a TV addict, a confidante, a raconteur, a bingo caller, a chaperone, a ballroom dancer, a caretaker, and more. I am expected to be a wonder-counsellor and a sympathetic ear, an entertaining orator and a man of profound depth. I am to be a "natural" with the young and patient with the old. I will acquire the wisdom of Solomon, the spirit of Elijah, the leadership of Moses, and the gentleness of Christ. And, in the meantime, I will be a dab hand at dealing with the drunken hecklers at Midnight Mass. I have, as a good friend often reminds me, an impossible job.

The demands made upon us as priests often seem unreasonable. In what other profession would you be expected to be on call twenty-four hours a day, seven days a week? How many doctors, or lawyers, or even teachers find themselves routinely being rung up about the most trifling of matters late into the evening or first thing in the morning? In what other career would highly qualified people be poorly paid and made to live on site all the time? To have any sort of a break the priest has to ensure he is physically unavailable; he has to refuse to answer the phone or door; he has to go away from his home and live somewhere else for a few days. People just cannot accept that he might be in the house but on holiday or off duty. Who else lives like that? The truth is, of course, that priesthood is not simply a profession or a career and that to think in those terms, however tempting, is quite misleading. Priesthood is a way of life – a way of living. For a fairer comparison I must look not only to the doctor, or lawyer, or teacher, but to the doctor with three teenage sons, the lawyer whose girlfriend has just left him, the teacher with a new wife, baby girl, and crippling mortgage. Who else is on call seven days a week, twenty-four hours a day? Anyone who has children, anyone in a serious relationship, anyone who is alive.

There is a tendency amongst priests to play the martyr. Our lives are stressful. Our pastoral ministry is quite un-relenting. We may often find ourselves feeling lonely and frustrated. We can become tired and feel unappreciated; but, then, so can anyone. The clergy are prone to bouts of self-pity. So many times I have joined in the "woe is me" conversations with other priests, as we lambast our parish-ioners for their demands and expectations and for failing to appreciate all we do. What utter nonsense such conversa-tions are when we stop to think about them. Yes, the "job" of being a priest working in a parish is hard; but the life of priesthood we have embraced is the way of our salvation. We would be the first to point out to any young couple that the difficulties and trials of their married life form part of the process in which they will learn to love as Christ. The same is ultimately true for the difficulties and trials of our priestly lives. And the reality is that, for most priests, life isn't that hard. Most priests I know take holidays abroad (often more than one a year). We don't have mortgages to worry about. It may be true that we live above the shop, but often – it has to be said – in pretty nice houses. Heating, food, council tax are all provided. Our salaries, though small for the level of our qualification and hours of work, are sufficient. We are known and respected in the local community. Generally, we are loved by our people. And the rewards of pastoral ministry can be quite humbling. We baptise babies and watch them grow up. We delve into (and try and stoke up) the love of young couples as we prepare them for their wedding days. We hand on our faith to converts and help them develop in their understanding of God. We have a window into the spiritual lives of our penitents and pronounce the forgiveness of their sins. We accompany our people through their difficult trials and are with them again in their happier times. We will pray with someone as they die and later conduct their funeral with love and dignity. Now what other profession boasts all this?

It strikes me, too, that, as we moan about the demands of our parish, we can sometimes overlook the demands we make on our parishioners. We count on them to turn out in all weathers to whatever services we happen to put on. We expect them to clean the church, and polish the brasses, and make the tea, and unlock the hall. We ask for musicians and readers and welcomers and Eucharistic ministers. We want flowers beautifully arranged and altar servers trained to a dignified regiment. This is just for the weekend liturgy. Let's not forget the rest of the week. Let's not forget the SVP who visit most of our sick and house bound, or the parish sisters who teach in our school and help with the RCIA, or the hospital volunteers who visit the wards for us, or the Open Door project that feeds our homeless, or the faithful who come in (usually unpaid) to answer the door and telephone so that Father can get on undisturbed with preparing his sermon, or writing his book, or watching his telly. And that's not to mention the parish council, the finance board, the social committee, and so on. All this and they have husbands or wives, and children and jobs, and friends and other commitments we might never know about. Yet still we're prone to moan: "This parish is supposed to be a community. I can't do everything by myself!"

Sometimes I think we priests forget one of the basic premises of the apostolic exhortation, *Christifideles Laici*: that the vineyard in which the laity are to labour is the vineyard of this modern world, with all "its problems and values, its unrest and hopes, its defeats and triumphs" (*CL* 3). A vineyard full of goodness, sincerity, honesty and truth but, sadly, also one in which the weeds of religious indifference and atheism are growing, in which the dignity of the human person is gradually being undermined, a place where humanity is "daily buffeted by conflict" (*CL* 4-6). It is in this world that the laity have their vocation to stand up and speak out and make a difference. "Through them, the Church of Christ is made present in the various sectors of the world, as a sign and source of hope and of love" (*CL* 7). Funnily enough, cleaning the brasses and polishing the floor, making the tea and answering the presbytery door all come second to that vital lay-ministry of continuing Christ's work of sanctification in the world. In other words, we clergy sometimes act as if our people have to be in the church building all week long to be considered good Christians. Yet, if we think about it, the very name of our principal liturgy, the Mass, comes from a Latin word meaning, to send out. The lay faithful are sent out from the Mass to fulfil their mission of building up God's kingdom in their married lives, in their families, at their work places, amongst friends, alongside colleagues, and even with strangers and people they've never met before. They have their own essential priestly dignity given to them through their baptism and are not dependent upon the jobs we tend to dole out (which are usually rather more about keeping the plant going and making sure the machinery remains well-oiled).

The Vatican II document, *Lumen Gentium*, talks about the ministerial priesthood differing from the common priesthood of the faithful at an essential level and not merely in degree (*LG* 10). Promoting such an ontological theology of priesthood (or "high" theology as some would daub it), although thoroughly rooted in Tradition, has fallen out of favour in recent years. I suspect that this has, in part at least, been a sop to those involved in promoting collaborative ministry – as if recognising differences or distinctions (especially ontological ones) somehow precludes working together. I also feel it is due to the poor ontological theology posited in the past: an "essential" theology of priesthood that became little other than a clerical apologetic. In reclaiming the ontology of orders the true meaning of *Lumen Gentium* needs to be examined. "Though they differ essentially and not only in degree, the common priesthood of the faithful and the ministerial priesthood or hierarchical priesthood are none the less ordered one to another" (*LG* 10). The last four words are important here. As priests we are changed at the essential level of being, not for our own sakes, but precisely for a new relationship with the rest of the baptised. Our priesthood is intimately and irrevocably linked to the common priesthood of the faithful because there is only one priesthood – that which belongs to Christ. As I have said earlier, through ordination the priest has taken on a public role, has become a sort of living sacrament: a showing forth and a making present of the true nature of the essential dignity of all who are baptised. We priests have become configured to Christ the Head, but this does not imply a decapitation from his Body, the community of the faithful.

It is this radical and new relationship with the people that I want to discuss in this chapter. If pastoral ministry is to be more than just the "job" of priests, then we need a theological framework in which to understand our interconnectedness with the laity. Just as in the chapter, *Prayer and Praise*, where I suggested that the priest's prayer – in virtue of his ordination – has been changed forever, so, too, I want to argue here that our relationship to others has been irreversibly remade. Antoine de Saint-Exupéry's little prince had to travel half way across the universe to learn the value of his relationship with his vain little rose. It can be sad to see priests floundering in their ministry and searching for some sort of meaning when part, at least, of such meaning is to be found right under their noses, in their day-to-day pastoral relationships. As *Presbyterorum Ordinis* says, "The priest, through the service of the people entrusted to his care and all the People of God, is able better to pursue the perfection of Christ, whose place he takes" (*PO* 12). In other words, for all of us baptised into Christ our fulfilment lies in those sentiments of St Paul writing to the Galatians: "It is no longer I who live, but Christ who lives in me" (Gal 2:20). For those of us configured to Christ the Head, through priestly ordination, such life can only come about if we are firmly connected to the rest of his Body. Again, as *Presbyterorum Ordinis* states, "Priests are configured to Christ the priest as servants of the Head, so that as co-workers with the episcopal order they may build up the body of Christ, the Church" (*PO* 12). There is clearly, in the teachings of Vatican II, the concept of a new relationship with Christ the High Priest (in virtue of presbyteral ordination) for the sake of (and, in effect, causing) a new relationship with the people. As this change is essential, or ontological, it affects our whole life purpose. As priests, we are created anew *for others*.

What, then, does this mean in practice? It means that our pastoral ministry is not an inconvenience to the rest of our priestly lives. A vision of priesthood that sees ministry as basically a weekend activity which luckily pays the bills and leaves the rest of the week free to go sailing, or collect butterflies, or play golf, or spend all our time shopping is a seriously blurred vision. It means, too, that priesthood is not some sort of selfish privilege, neither to be guarded and closeted away, nor paraded with superior vanity and clerical pride. More blurred vision would be seeing priestly life as some sort of purely personal path to holiness. Even in a Trappist community, those who are called to be priests embark upon a new life of ministry for their brother monks. Ministry – engagement with the people of God at a radical level – is to be at the very heart of our newly created identities. I remember once, in the seminary as a student, asking one of the staff to sign my passport photograph. On the form he had to write down his relationship to me. I assumed he would write "lecturer" or "teacher." In fact, he wrote "pastor." I remember it because I recall thinking at the time, as I left his study, "Yes, you have been a pastor to me; you have ministered to my needs." And I know now that it was his ministry to me – his role as pastor – that inspired me as a student and not, in fact, his grasp of Old Testament theology (good as it undoubtedly was).

This theology of orders also captures something of the essence of God himself. Priestly service is to be an expression (but not the only one) of that ecstatic, divine Love which freely chooses others. A Love that created all there is, even though in its inner, Trinitarian dynamic, it was completely self-sufficient. A Love that chose to redeem a fallen world even at the cost of the humiliation of the cross. A Love which is freely outpoured, which freely predisposes itself for the other. Priesthood, too, is to be directed outwards, in terms of service. This is one reason, I think, why the rule of celibacy has been imposed upon the majority of the presbyterate in the west: to draw out the sign of that selfless love and service which is to be the soul of our pastoral ministry. It also draws out the notion of partnership. In the Catholic Church in the UK – at least in my parish – there is a strong sense of allegiance. I quite naturally speak of "my people" and I often hear the laity referring to "our priests." Celibacy enables this relationship to be highlighted somewhat but the actual bond is fundamental to priesthood itself. I am ordained and sent to them, the people of St Mary's, to be their priest. I occasionally think of it in terms of the comedy duo, Morecambe and Wise. When, sadly, Eric Morecambe died so too, in effect, did Ernie Wise's career. They were partners whose professional lives had been bound up together. The relationship of priest and laity is a similar partnership. We are bound up together. I am to be caught up in the lives of my people. Without someone to minister to, I am hardly a minister. My first year as a priest was spent studying, shut up in a seminary in Rome. Initially I found it quite hard. What was the point of my being ordained if I had no ministry to exercise? Then my spiritual director at the time told me to think about my ministry for those in the community. "Minister to them in simple ways. Pray for them. You must pray for them, especially the guys you don't like. Make the effort to get along. Be generous." I began to do this, and "bigger" ministry in fact evolved. It struck me, then, that however little ministry there is "to do," there are always relationships to be had. It seems, just as with our prayer, that there is the risk of overly focusing on what we do and on how we do it, rather than on what we are. We are priests for others.

It is this relationship within pastoral ministry that is important. Quite early on in my ministry I was called upon to accompany spiritually a woman in her early forties from the day she was diagnosed with cancer to the day before she died. I remember getting the phone call from her, at about six o'clock in the evening. She was weepy and incoherent and needed to speak to a priest. We had never met before, as I'd only just arrived in the parish. My car journey to her house (some eight miles away) was the beginning of a journey that would last just over a year. She was lucky in that she had around her a supportive family and plenty of good friends. But she wanted the priest, from time to time, because she wanted to celebrate sacramentally all that Christ was doing in her. Each time we met we would celebrate the sacraments of reconciliation, anointing, and Eucharist, and have a fairly extended period of prayer in which she would simply commend to her Lord those she loved. Those moments have been amongst the most potent and moving prayer-moments of my life. My role, as well as being yet another figure of support, was principally to enable her to see God working in her life and suffering. It was a challenge, certainly, but it was also a privilege – a privilege I only received because I was her priest at that time.

I have, too, in my pastoral ministry accompanied people on all sorts of other journeys, or at least parts of journeys. I have married any number of couples and tried to help them prepare for their married lives. I often smile to myself, nowadays, when I realise that at the start of my time in Yarmouth most couples used to be about my age, whereas five years later I tend to be a little older than them. The rewarding element of marriage preparation is that, usually, I find myself becoming friends with those I will marry. I admit that every year I have "favourite" couples. But I think – whether or not we hit it off and become friends – that the relationship is important. It is the relationship between someone configured to Christ the servant-king, and two people he came to serve. I have baptised I don't know how many babies and young children during my time here in Yarmouth. On some occasions I have found myself baptising the child of a couple I married two or so years earlier, and whose grandmother (or other relative) I may have buried six months before. I have also watched teenagers grow up and become interesting young adults. I have been privy to their relationship failures and their latest loves (as well as to their changing musical tastes and fashion fads). I have instructed and received into the Church quite a few adults, and been inspired by their love of God and the often amazing ways in which they have been led to him. I have "been there" for all sorts of all ages of people. I have done this – and had the chance to do this – because I am their priest. I am caught up in the most intimate parts of people's lives, which is one of the great joys and fulfilment of pastoral ministry, and I have grown immeasurably because of it.

There are three words that can never escape attention in any serious discussion on the priesthood, both common and ministerial. Through the sacraments of initiation we are, all of us, configured to Christ, priest, prophet and king. Through the sacrament of orders, priests are configured anew – but to the same Christ who is still priest, prophet, and king. What, then, at a pastoral level does this really mean? Actually I think it is quite hard to divide those three areas of Christian ministry, since they overlap so much. Perhaps the easiest approach is to examine the Mass. In the gathered assembly of the faithful the ordained priest stands vested as a symbol of Christ in their midst. Christ is, of course, already present in their very gathering. One of the functions of the ordained minister is to point to that already existing reality. In the prayers of the liturgy often the priest prays aloud but alone with hands extended. This is the symbol of the priestly nature of those prayers, uttered on behalf of all present. They are not the priest's own prayer: they are the prayers of the priestly people of God. In the Liturgy of the Word, through the homily, the priest attempts to incarnate in the lives of his people the Word of God who is already present through the proclamation of the Scriptures. The ordained minister is exercising a prophetic role by trying to enunciate how the Word of God, just celebrated, is actually abiding in the lives of those gathered. Preaching is such a difficult task – and such an important one – because it doesn't merely rely on a good knowledge of Scripture and a good technique of oratory (although these, too, are invaluable) but it demands a knowledge of how Christ is speaking to his people at the present moment. The priest can only really know this if he is tuned into the Word of God through his own personal life and prayer, through his other sacramental celebrations (especially the sacrament of reconciliation), and through his overall pastoral care and involvement in the lives of his parishioners. Fortunately (and we must never forget this) the Holy Spirit plays a pretty leading role in our preaching, and often we will speak to peoples' hearts in ways we could never even imagine. Finally, in the gathering together of the people for the celebration of Mass, and in the blessing and sending of them back to the awaiting world, the priest exercises a kingly – or I prefer to say shepherding – role. Through his ministry a diverse people are brought together to celebrate and recognise their royal dignity as the people of God. Through the celebration of Word and Sacrament, those people are enabled to return to the world sustained and fed, forgiven and re-created, so as to continue their day-to-day ministry of bringing about the kingdom of God. "Go in peace, to love and serve the Lord" is the command of the shepherd-priest to his flock of kingly-sheep at the end of such celebration. In the Mass, then, the ordained priest is at once priest, prophet and king but only so as to point to and make present the priestly, prophetic, and kingly nature of his assembled people.

The role and scope of pastoral priests can be described in lots of ways. We have embarked upon a life of sacramental ministry, most obviously. We have the duty to celebrate with our people the sacraments entrusted to the Church. We are called, also, to a ministry of mission: of proclaiming (and living out) the message of *hesed* which we find promised in the Old Testament, and which we see fulfilled in the annunciation of *Emmanuel* with the coming of Christ; of witnessing to the reality of the resurrection, and the unlimited, unwavering hope that it offers a fallen world; of promoting mercy, justice, and compassion in all that we do.

A while ago I was at a Christmas lunch of the Jesus Caritas fraternity in my diocese and we had convened in a local pub for a meal and a few drinks. There were the usual tacky, paper, seasonal serviettes in red and green with reindeer and holly all over them. There were also a few candles stuck in empty wine bottles, which the waitress was having difficulty lighting. "Give them here," said one of my colleagues, "candles are our stock in trade," and he had them all lit in a moment. I began to wonder (as you do, when your mind is more on the book you're writing than the company you're keeping) what exactly is our stock in trade as priests? What, at a day-to-day level and more than anything else, am I asked to deal with in pastoral ministry? The answer is, I think, sin. At every Mass I pray for the forgiveness of sins. I tell of the blood of that new and eternal covenant which will be poured out for all so that sins may be forgiven. Every Saturday I sit in a box and listen for an hour to penitents confessing their sins and seeking reconciliation. On Sunday afternoons I baptise young children, freeing them from the shackles of original sin. During the week I may celebrate any number of times the sacrament of the sick, where I pray for healing but also for the forgiveness of sins. In my pastoral counselling and spiritual direction, although I may avoid using the word, most of what we discuss sooner or later boils down to sin. In my dealings with the poor and the needy, more often than not, I come across examples of structural sin, of victims of sin, of people caught up in a sinful world. This might seem rather negative. What, though, is sin if not a turning away from God at some level or another? And the reality is – for most of us – that we have, at least in part, turned away. Our whole life journey consists in being persuaded to turn back around; to face Him and to realise that all we will actually encounter is simply Love itself. It seems to me that most of my priestly, pastoral ministry is ultimately about being privileged to be a part of that ongoing, divine persuasion.

In many ways I do have an impossible job. The demands and expectations are sometimes simply too much. If only more of my parish had read the words of *Presbyterorum Ordinis*, which speaks of their obligations to treat me with filial love, to share my anxieties, to help me – as far as possible – in the carrying out of my duties (*PO* 9). Some hope, I suppose. But, of course, just as with my prayer, my pastoral ministry is more than simply a job. Being a priest is ultimately what I am, and not what I do. My life, now, is to be lived for others. It is to be lived, not begrudgingly, but in love. And the challenge remains here too: the challenge to avoid becoming the pastoral professional; the challenge to try and be someone for others.

INSTITUTIONS AND STRUCTURES

BEFORE I write anything else in this chapter I need to write the following: it was the institutional Church which took me, twelve years ago, a young man somewhat lacking in confidence (but, I suppose, with three half-decent A-levels) and has produced what I am today. It was the structures and institutions of this same Church (and the good people working within them) which have given me confidence in myself, have educated me to the highest level of my capabilities, have enabled me (and asked me) to fulfil a number of ambitions and dreams, have provided me with my living, my job, my security, and above all which have opened up the horizons of my faith and fostered in me an ever deepening love of God. A Church which has undoubtedly challenged me; which certainly frustrates me; but which nevertheless has formed me. A Church – institutional and structured – to which I owe a lot and for which I am truly grateful.

It is well known – at least amongst students of ecclesiology – that, in their discussions on the constitution of the Church at Vatican II, the Council Fathers rejected a first draft of the document that was to become *Lumen Gentium* because it was too juridical and institutional. According to Kevin McNamara in his book, *The Church*, the original schema proposed eleven chapters, five of which dealt to a large degree with the episcopacy, priesthood, religious life, and authority, three of which concerned the visible, institutional structures of the Church, and only one chapter each dealing with the laity, ecumenism, and the call to preach the gospel. Just looking at the titles of each of these proposed chapters betrays the extent to which the pre-conciliar Church was pyramidal and overly-clerical in its self-understanding. The original schema presented a Church as a visible, perfect society in which the Pope was at the top, with the bishops, priests, and then religious fanning out below him, underneath which were the laity; a Church which was organised, authoritative, oh, and preached the gospel too! Thankfully, the Spirit was at work and such a simplistic vision was rejected by the Council in favour of the much richer mystery portrayed in *Lumen Gentium*. But today, in our post-conciliar world, I sometimes wonder just how much the attitudes of that original draft document still prevail – even among young clergy like myself.

These days "collaborative ministry" is the catch phrase, but like any form of words it is pretty meaningless until put into action. We can all too easily bandy about buzz words such as "collaboration" and "dialogue" whilst still exercising a rather monarchical, monological ministry. I can think of a parish that voices the collaborative dream and has recently set up teams of lay visitors and Eucharistic ministers under the remit of the parish priest. All very politically correct, except to note that in the same parish the St Vincent de Paul Society has been completely sidelined. The group which has its own core spirituality and autonomy, its own history and well tried practices of visiting and care for the poor, has been effectively replaced with a pastoral strategy of the pastor's own devising. Collaboration or control freakery? *Koinonia* or good old-fashioned authoritarianism? Another example is of a "new model parish" jointly run (in effect) by a parish priest and a parish sister. When a student friend of mine went there for a year on placement, he found himself presented with a "pastoral covenant" which he had to sign. It was basically one of the most outrageous and uncollaborative contracts I had ever seen. No one sat down with him to discuss the pastoral needs of the area. No one asked him about where he felt his strengths and weaknesses lay. He was simply told to do this and to do that – all, of course, couched in the language of team work. Again, is this collaboration? Or is it rather an example of delegating to the new boy the "rubbish" jobs that the others don't like doing? The problem with collaboration is that it means "to work with" rather than "to work for." To work with, to be joint partners in the mission of spreading the Good News is a huge challenge for any of us. How much easier to persuade people "to work for" our vision, our mission – especially if we can wrap it up in the language of *communio*. Perhaps this is where the Church is going awry in this country. We seem to be interpreting collaborative ministry as the engagement of the laity in the work of the clergy, but there's no way we'll let the laity in on the real decision making processes. Stick a few of them on a diocesan commission or two, get them to do the parish visiting, make them all Eucharistic ministers – but hand them a parish cheque book, or let them make a real decision? Never!

All this belies the reality that, for all our recent documents such as *Christifideles Laici* and *The Sign We Give*, we are still pretty much a pyramidal institution. This is never more evident than amongst the ranks of the clergy themselves. Just looking at my agenda for the next diocesan Council of Priests, it is striking how almost every item for discussion comes from either the vicar-general or the bishop. Now I don't want to blame the vicar-general or the bishop for this fact. I am aware that it is partly due to the reticence of the rest of us. Whenever the bishop looks to set up a subcommittee, all heads go down and there's an eerie silence in which you just know that every man is praying for himself. But it suggests to me that we are failing as clergy to collaborate – to work together. At the deanery and diocesan level we have our pecking order; and back in our parishes we set up our own little pyramids – with ourselves firmly at the top.

In the previous chapter I examined how, through ordination, the priest enters into a radically new relationship with his people. This newness ought to be most visible when it comes to our relationship with other clergy. Upon ordination as deacon we are incardinated into a diocese and then, as priest, we enter the order of the presbyterate. In the actual ordination rite itself this is expressed with the kiss of peace. There is a new bond which unites those of us in the priesthood – we are sharing in a new way in the one priesthood of Christ. My brother once remarked to me: "It seems now as if you have two families – us, and your fellow priests." In one sense he is right. There is a bond which unites us within a diocese – a bond of fraternity as we express the priestly vocation of the whole of the local Church and share the concern for its mission. However, this sense of fraternity or family – this bond which unites us – is far removed from the notion of a gentleman's club which sadly the presbyterate can so easily become; a sort of stuffy, paternalistic common room. After six years of ordination, I'm afraid I am a little tired of diocesan celebrations that are supposed to foster and express brotherhood and yet merely reinforce the clerical pyramid. I have had enough of notions of clerical fraternity that are little more than networking, or simply an excuse for a parish financed junket. I am aware that the call to fraternity for me personally is quite a challenge. I am essentially quite a shy man. I don't really like change. I am young. Most of my brother priests are considerably older than me and I often think to myself, "What do we have in common?" The answer, I know, is Christ's priesthood. But that theological statement doesn't make having lunch with priests I've hardly met before any easier. It doesn't enable me to adapt any better to the changed circumstances of presbytery life when a new parish priest arrives, or a third priest comes to stay for a while. I am rather sensitive to being patronised too. This isn't helped by well meaning clerics referring to me as "the boy" or "young Sean" and treating me kindly, but as if I'd only just stopped wearing short trousers. I am thirty-two and more than aware of what I might be doing in life if I wasn't a priest. Suffering such paternalism with a smile and good grace doesn't come easily to me at all. I do have priest friends, of course, both within the diocese and elsewhere around the country – and these people are an essential support to me in my life and ministry. But the challenge of fraternity is to be prepared to become a support for others, even those I find difficult or don't much like. I am all too painfully aware that this is one of the areas of my ministry that is largely neglected precisely because I find it so demanding.

One of the most striking examples of the pyramid model of Church still being in force, despite all our protestations of *koinonia*, is at the Chrism Mass. Here, just before the celebration of the Triduum, the local Church gathers together. Naturally, the bishop presides over us all. But in my diocese he has a sort of panel of presiders with him: the vicar-general, the chancellor, the cathedral administrator (and anyone else vaguely considered "important") with a couple of deacons either side – all fanning out from him in rank order. Then, tucked away near the choir, the rest of the presbyterate. And the people? Squashed in behind the "concelebrating" permanent deacons and the Knights of the Holy Sepulchre; stuck behind the great grey pillars unable to see a thing. I ask myself each year: is this Mass supposed to be a symbol of *communio* or a clerical rally? I heard a liturgist once remark, "We are what we celebrate." Sadly, how true this is: we are still the pyramid.

The pyramid is evident in other ways too. The trips of our current Holy Father, Pope John Paul II, around the world – although very good in many ways – seem to carry with them the unfortunate side effect of promoting his ministry as some sort of super-bishop of the world. What could and should have been presented as the successor of St Peter travelling to re-affirm and to support the local Churches and his brother bishops has been misunderstood and misrepresented in terms of triumphalistic rallies and assertions of Papal authority. What is so striking is the way the Papal insignia replaces any and all insignia of the local

Church. Even at the symbolic level what comes across is not affirmation but domination. Vatican II spoke about a collegiality amongst the bishops, based upon the Petrine ministry of unity. As we enter the third millennium, the common perception – from both Catholics and non-Catholics alike – is one of the Pope as an arch-archbishop standing over and above the others; a sort of universally reigning monarch.

This pyramidal presentation is found within the Vatican itself. Departments are headed by cardinals and archbishops and staffed by monsignors and priests. The question surely has to be asked: why? Why do we need an archbishop to head a bureaucratic department? Why do I need to carry the title monsignor in order to open the Pope's postbag? Why so few lay-workers at any important level? Why such a clerical, pyramidal management structure? Whatever happened to collaboration and *koinonia*? The cynic in me would say that priests cost a lot less to employ and are easier to control. Recruiting the same level of highly educated lay-staff would actually cost a fortune. Furthermore, they wouldn't be bound by obedience. Practical excuses, I suppose, but ones that lead to a pyramidal practice.

Diocesan structures are less clerical, at least in my diocese, but the pyramid still tends to prevail. The laity that do find themselves with influence are usually drawn from groupies based around one or other of the more senior priests of the diocese. There is no serious recruitment and theological training of lay-people. Again, this would all cost money. Rather, people are co-opted onto committees and boards in an ad hoc way. The third millennium, we are told, will be the millennium of the laity in the Church – but there appears to be no serious planning or preparation to enable such a reality to come about. The danger is, of course, that without any real leadership and direction the parishes of the future will simply be dominated by the most articulate and middle class families that live in them, and the liturgy will be directed by the already overworked teachers from the local primary school. As I see it, this needn't be the case. At local and diocesan level, it would make much more sense to be preparing now for lay-leadership: providing any number of schemes to draw young people into pastoral practice (without it having to be a back door way of tempting them to ordination or religious vows); encouraging serious catechesis and promoting adult theological study (and not just RCIA courses and the odd Bible study day); recruiting and training laity in the exercise of their appropriate ministries. The problem is that this all involves a huge investment of time and money, and it demands vision and leadership.

Collaboration, it seems to me, is more than mere delegation, which is just as well since I am rubbish at delegation. It is actually about involving the laity in the mission of the local Church – and that means drawing upon their ideas, listening to their vision; together trying to discern the Word of God speaking to our communities. But I am aware that this is so difficult. It assumes that we listen to one another, and not merely pursue our own agenda. It presupposes that we are all of us tuned into what "the Spirit is saying to the churches" (Rev 2:7), and not simply there with our own particular axe to grind. My fear is that it will result in endless boring meetings and for that reason I sometimes do not collaborate. I know that on occasions it will mean my viewpoint will need to take a back seat and so, again, I often go it alone. One area in my own ministry where I do feel collaboration has worked is in my school chaplaincy. For a number of years now I have been involved part time in a large, mixed comprehensive school. Although fairly flexible, the basic structure in which I work has always involved a number of lay-people (both teaching staff and volunteers) who have taken on co-ordinating roles, have been engaged in liturgical preparation and celebration, have ministered to students and fellow staff at a one-to-one level, and who have come together as a team to share ideas, to support one another, and to carry forward a vision of how best to promote the school's Christian ethos. My own part in this team has changed over the years. Now, as the longest serving team member, I do co-ordinate the rest of the team more; but it wasn't always this way. As the priest, clearly, I have taken the prominent role in liturgical celebration – presiding, preaching, and guiding the overall style of liturgy which the school celebrates. But as a team we have striven to give the staff and students a deeper understanding of how to celebrate – of what liturgy actually means. The success of such an approach has been evident on a number of occasions where students have voluntarily produced their own para-liturgies. They have begun to understand and articulate the need for communal prayer and for celebrating lives imbued with God's presence. I, too, have been engaged in one-to-one ministry with people in need in the school but I have always felt carried and supported by the rest of the team. There has been a real interchange of ideas; a real dialogue in how best to pursue pastoral practice. And, it being a school, I, as the priest, haven't wielded the cheque book. Interestingly, there has never really evolved a pyramid; we simply work together; we simply collaborate.

Reflecting upon my school experience it strikes me that collaboration has worked because I have not been placed upon – or been allowed to place myself upon – the clerical pedestal. We are a small team and we work together quite closely. We see each other tired and stressed out. We have disagreements sometimes, and arguments sometimes, but always the one thing that unites us is our chaplaincy role within the school. There is no time for status. I think one of the obstacles to collaboration within parishes is still that pedestal. The majority of people in the parish only see the priest on a Sunday and only see him "doing" holy things such as celebrating Mass. However human we are, however warm and loving and approachable we strive to become, most people only see us at our best; most people only see a fraction of our ministry and lives. And what they see is this:

we wear different clothes; we use titles such as "Father" or "Monsignor" or "Canon"; we live in the Church (admittedly, next door – but the people mostly see us in Church); we talk about God; we read the Scriptures; we preach the Good News. The assumption is always going to be that somehow we manage to live the gospel more fully than they do. It is a false assumption, to be sure, but a tempting one to believe even ourselves. So naturally enough our people place us upon a pedestal whether we like it or not (and the fact is that sometimes we do rather like it). And then we try to encourage them to be partners with us in building up the kingdom of God. It is too late. Already the pyramid is well under construction.

One of the more disconcerting aspects of the movement towards collaborative ministry is the reaction against it by some of our newer priests. Just as there seems to be a reaction against so many other "politically correct" notions, so seminarians these days appear to be tiring of the *koinonia* mantra. This isn't helped by the uncollaborative way in which seminaries conduct themselves. The academic staffing of these institutions is almost totally clerical, with maybe a token layman or lay-woman as a pastoral director or something. There is always the suspicion (usually unfounded) by some students of another agenda, especially if the lay-staff member is a woman. She probably wants to be a priest, is the common assumption. "Why hasn't she got a real job?" is the unarticulated question. And there is the rather spurious fear that maybe, somehow, she has got the rest of the "liberal" staff firmly under her thumb. When I hear stories of seminaries considering making their course on the Eucharist optional to the theology degree in favour of the three compulsory courses on team ministry and the like, then I see why students fear that hidden agenda. No wonder seminaries these days are tending to produce reactionary right-wingers. But, of course, such stories are usually just further scare tactics by those same reactionaries. What really bothers me is why more laity aren't involved on the academic staff in the first place. Get away from tokenism; bring in decent, well-educated lay-staff across the board, and maybe then the right-wing paranoia will go away.

In my own time in seminary, we had a rector who used to use the phrase, "the wider community." What he actually meant was the domestic staff. At one stage we were invited to collaborate in the writing of the seminary's mission statement. At the same time – by coincidence – we were banned from discussing the issue of food at the staff-student meetings, which were held once a term. Now in my day the food was truly awful (it's better since, I believe) but no one was prepared to do anything about it. I used to wonder, what actually affects the community more: the food we eat, or some abstract set of words that will be stuck in the front of a prospectus? Why are we invited to work together on the latter but not to improve the former? For all the language of community and "wider community" there was no real collaboration on the things that actually mattered to us at a day-to-day level. Until seminaries as institutions become truly collaborative, I don't see how students will be convinced to pursue such enlightened models of ministry themselves once ordained.

Another barrier to the exercise of a truly collaborative ministry is the laity itself. In my experience, the level of catechesis amongst Catholics is pretty poor. How can we begin to invite dialogue and shared ministry when the average parishioner hasn't a clue what we're talking about? How can we start to "work with" the people, when their expectations of priests has only ever been "to work for" Father? The pyramidal model is too ingrained in our psyches to be dismissed overnight. For *Lumen Gentium*, for *Christifideles Laici*, for *The Sign We Give* and all the other good and worthy teachings to become a reality in our parishes in this country, a lot more time is needed, a lot more catechesis is demanded, and a lot more faith from the hierarchy is required that this really is the way forward.

There is an inevitable tension in an institutional Church

84

that at one moment invites lay-participation and collaboration whilst at the same time asserts itself as hierarchical. One thorny issue is, of course, the question of the ordination of women priests. Since the concept of governance in the Church is clearly laid at the door of the ordained ministry and nowhere else, how can women ever (short of being ordained) come to exercise any real authority? How can the Church ever move on from being male-dominated? And yet, if we look to the early Church (when the theology of orders was not so worked out) we do have clear examples of women taking positions of leadership – governing roles – within the Church. Perhaps one of the controversies to be settled in this millennium will be the role of the laity in the area of ecclesial leadership. Perhaps one of the developments in our understanding of priesthood and in our model of ministry will be to move away from the need to have a clerical dominance in the arena of Church governance. Perhaps, then, with lay leadership – and women in positions of real authority – the pressure for ordination of women might die away, and true collaboration might begin to take hold.

CELIBACY AND SEXUALITY

IN NOVEMBER last year Niamh, my niece, was born. It had been something of an anxious time for my brother and his partner because the pregnancy hadn't been altogether routine, but in the end everything was okay. This year the family went through a similar experience with another of my brothers and his wife. And this time the baby – Michael – was born a month premature, by coincidence falling exactly on the day of Niamh's first birthday. Again in the event everything was fine. Oddly, these occasions have had a strange effect on me. Seeing my two brothers with their new, firstborn children; watching them cope with the demands of fatherhood; sharing in their sheer pride: this has all made me think. Niamh's birth was not the first time I had become an uncle – my oldest brother has a teenage boy and a girl. But I suppose that when my oldest nephew was born I was only fifteen myself and so the prospect of my having children wasn't honestly on the horizon. This time, though, it is different: this time, when I hold little Michael or play with young Niamh, something pulls at my heart strings. If I wasn't celibate, I think to myself, this could be my son or my daughter.

These feelings remind me of something that happened shortly after I was first ordained a deacon – remind me of an image which, up until now, I have successfully repressed. I was walking through a park one Sunday afternoon with another student for the priesthood and a religious sister. I expect we were engaged in erudite discussion – or more likely we were chatting Church politics. Whichever, we were interrupted when a man about my age (mid twenties at the time) cut across our path, holding the hand of a four or five year old girl who was skipping happily alongside him. She held a little, wrapped up parcel and they were obviously on their way somewhere. As our conversation continued I began a slightly depressed daydream. This is how I should be spending my Sunday afternoons, I thought to myself. Not talking shop with two celibates, but taking my daughter to a kid's party: doing something "normal".

In all the years of priestly formation and preparation I suppose most of the tension surrounding celibacy – for me at least – centred on sex and intimacy. We were given talks about exclusive relationships and about the differences of repression and suppression. We read books on sexuality and the celibate life – some more psychoanalytical than others, but none particularly helpful late at night. We had moral theology seminars on masturbation and sexual intercourse. But no one ever suggested that one day I would want to be a father; that one day I would want to be "normal".

The challenge of celibacy is perennial. It is constantly throwing up new questions and demanding newer and ever more relevant answers to existing ones. Sexuality and sex, intimacy and friendship, procreation and parenthood, loneliness and aloneness, self-image: these are just some of the issues to be addressed. But the celibate's consolation is that this list applies to anyone who is seriously committed to authentic loving. A husband and wife face equal challenges in all the same areas. A celibate life is no harder than a married one. We are essentially in the same arena – it's just that sometimes we're not always fighting exactly the same lion. This is something I have to remind myself when I'm caught indulging in a self-pitying craving for normalcy. Wanting a "normal" life – which I often do – is merely wanting an easy life, and who has one of those?

One of the difficulties of dealing with celibacy is that the struggles we encounter are so often solitary struggles.

Unsurprisingly, most diocesan priests are not in the business of pouring out their celibate woes to their parishioners, nor even to their colleagues within the diocese. As a rule, we priests just don't talk about our celibate lives – or not, at least, until something goes horribly wrong. Our celibacy is caught up with our sexuality and is deeply personal and private. And yet, in my experience, it does help to have someone – be it a spiritual director, a regular confessor, or a trusted friend – in which to confide; someone with whom to be oneself. Part of this problem of seclusion comes from the practice of celibacy itself: we cannot express ourselves through our sexuality as we might because people assume and expect us to be asexual. We have taken a promise which sets us apart and being set apart can be quite lonesome at times.

A related problem is the language we use. To share your intimate feelings with the one you love – the object of those feelings – and who you know loves you is one thing. To try and express similar intimate yearnings to a third party in a similarly intimate way is quite another. How does a priest begin to tell someone that he is eaten up by loneliness every night, or that he has fallen madly in love with the parish treasurer's wife, or that he thinks he might be gay, or that he finds himself trawling through the telly channels in search of something mildly erotic? How does he talk about such things without embarrassment and in a language that really expresses what he feels? Impure thoughts, self-abuse, breaking the sixth and ninth commandments – these terms don't even begin to scratch the surface of our real sexual and emotional longings.

There are, of course, numerous books on the market dedicated to the subject and, indeed, some are very good. But again it is often a question of language. Subjects are couched in such delicate phrases or hedged around to such an extent that sometimes you wonder at their relevance. Statistics and psychology are employed in a way that makes you feel yourself simply a number or a category. In the six years of my priesthood, and in the six years before that of my training for priesthood, I have longed to read something – or to listen to someone's talk – which echoed my own experience and my own feelings.

This chapter, then, is written hesitantly and from the point of view of failure. Hesitantly, because what can I add to what has already been written? Hesitantly, because how can I succeed in using a language that I feel others do not use? It is written from the point of view of failure because from the outset I freely admit that I am a failed celibate. This chapter is not an attempt to provide an answer: how to be celibate successfully. It is not even a type of self-help: learn from my mistakes. It is simply a set of honest reflections upon my own celibacy and sexuality, in the light of the theology of vocation and priestly ordination that I have already outlined.

A few years ago a leading Anglican churchman made quite an unusual statement to awaiting journalists and TV cameras. He acknowledged that his sexuality was rather a grey area. There were, needless to say, reasons for such a public admission but these aren't what interest me now. What does interest me is that very concept of sexual identity. A fact facing every celibate is that to most people we are a sexual enigma. If I was married with three children my heterosexuality would be assured, there for all to see. If I was gay and living with my partner again my status would be known. But as a celibate how can people judge me? Am I asexual? That I promise you I am not. So what am I? As celibate priests we have to live with jokes about choir boys and sneers about paedophiles; we find ourselves being flirted with by (usually) older women who (definitely) ought to know better; we are placed upon pedestals – or we place ourselves there – as martyrs to our God, having supposedly given up sexuality altogether. Perhaps at worst our celibacy makes no impact on anyone at all: we are simply an irrelevance, an anachronism in the modern world. Whatever the truth of our sexual past and present, we remain for many a "grey" area.

This difficulty with expression of sexual identity is well illustrated by students' behaviour in seminary. In my time I have lived and have been a part of the communities of two major seminaries, and I have spoken to students and priests from a number of others where the story is still the same. A group of forty or more men, pretty much all in their mid twenties to early thirties, living closely together, studying together, striving to be celibate. Even as we enter the third millennium, there is very little contact with women and still less with married people or young courting couples. And so, in a rather intense and sexually abnormal environment, there evolves within the seminary different broad groups. There is usually quite a macho brigade, always regaling the community with tales of former girlfriends as they march off to play football with the "lads". There is also a correspondingly more effeminate group whose humour, although quick-witted, is often dulled by an incessant camp tone. There are the gin and lace crowd, and the jogging and cold showers lot. There are those who develop a string of different friends – men and women – outside the community, and those who shut themselves away. What unites us all is that we are struggling to show (or not to show) our sexual identity. It would be crass to suggest that the football players were all straight while the gin and lace group were all homosexual. But it doesn't take a psychologist to realise that dressing up statues of Our Lady, or taking inordinate amounts of exercise, or expending energy on liturgical garments, or boring people rigid about past relationships aren't – at least in part – really about projecting a sexuality. Whether the message we are trying to project is in fact the truth is one thing. Whether we ourselves, at that stage in our lives, even know the truth is yet another.

Whatever the reality of our sexuality – however black and white, or grey, we may find ourselves – there is usually some sort of sexual and emotional growth to be found in the process of making and learning to sustain loving relationships. But for the celibate priest – whatever his actual orientation – there is the added complication of not being able to express his sexuality in the ordinary ways. I don't mean that someone can only mature sexually through genital behaviour but I do believe that people grow through affective interaction: learning to channel their emotions, their inclinations; learning to love others; experiencing the life-enhancing feeling of reciprocation. In other words, our intimate relationships can themselves be a school in which to grow in sexual and self-understanding. Celibacy doesn't preclude these things but it does raise certain challenges: if I am celibate how do I learn to deal with my sexuality? How do I discover my true inclinations? To whom do I tell my intimate longings? Where do I experience being loved as another sexual being? Similarly, if the priest entered seminary at a young age (as I did), he may have missed out on some pretty basic experiences: a one to one relationship, falling in love, the first kiss. There is a danger, then, that celibacy actually becomes a refuge: a way of refusing to admit or to face up to one's sexual proclivities. It may even be a safe place: somewhere to avoid the challenges of growing up. In the black and white world – if there is such a thing – of human sexual development, celibacy can become a very grey area indeed.

One of the best things that ever happened to me during my preparation for the priesthood – and also one of the most painful – was falling in love. I entered the seminary aged twenty, pretty straight-laced and fairly emotionally buttoned up. Just over half way through my training I met someone and we gradually became emotionally and intimately involved. My world was turned upside down. Here was I eighteen months away from making a promise of celibacy and I was madly in love. What was perhaps even more disturbing was that someone actually loved me. At last – not just as a friend, or a family member, or as an exercise in the virtue of charity – someone loved me for how I looked, and how I spoke, and what I did; someone wanted to be with me. I felt alive. It still makes me smile now to think about some of the corny ways in which we showed one another affection. We were a young couple in love and so were acting just like any other besotted young couple. Sadly it didn't last long and that is when the pain began. We broke up because I decided, after a lot of heart wrenching and soul searching, that I did have a vocation and that I still wanted to be a priest. I was fortunate to have a wise spiritual director at the time who supported me throughout and who kept coming back to me with the refrain: "Where is Jesus Christ in all of this?" Through that experience I grew immeasurably in self-understanding and in an awareness of the potency of my sexuality. I also gained an insight into the workings of new love: romantic, silly, intense, sexually charged, exciting, absorbing. And that insight has been a useful pastoral tool in my priestly ministry ever since.

It strikes me that to be prepared and able to accept celibacy for the sake of the kingdom (Cf. Mt 19:12) it might be of benefit to make some theological reflections on the meaning of our sexual natures. This is not to say that we will find our sexual identity in academics and exegesis but we can discover in Scripture the image of who we are meant to be. Certainly in the UK, and probably in the West in general, we are immersed in a culture that is obsessed with sex and shopping. The two are most obviously intertwined in some of the clever advertisements we see on the telly. Drink Nescafé Goldblend and the chances are you'll have a whirlwind romance with the girl who lives downstairs. Upgrade your car to a Peugeot 306 and you'll experience a corresponding upgrade in your libido and quite an enhanced performance in your marital love life. This is, of course, all complete nonsense but nevertheless advertisers have cottoned on to the fact that sex sells. One of my own personal fears about my celibate life is that sometimes I have only taken the sex element out of the equation (and even that is not completely excised). Far from being – along with fruitful and fulfilled Christian married couples – a living sign of the true meaning of sexuality and human love, I have fallen for the adverts. In a world where we are told that everyone is shopping and having sex, I am busy shopping and wishing I was having sex. Mind you, I suspect that this is the reality for a lot of non-celibates too.

I don't want to berate our current age as some terrible time where commercialism and sexual promiscuity rule the roost. We are actually no different from any other age. The roots of modern materialism (and sexual practices which treat sex as just another commodity are a type of materialism) lie deep in the history of humanity itself: indeed, they are to be found in our understanding of the first sin of Adam. If we turn to the book of Genesis we see in both creation accounts (Gen 1:1-2, 4a and 2:4b-25) an envisaged balance and harmony. "Let us make man in our own image, in the likeness of ourselves," says God; and so we are told, "male and female he created them" (Gen 1:26-27). "It is not good that man should be alone," says the Lord; and we are told that God fashioned woman from one of Adam's ribs, so that she might be "bone of my bone and flesh of my flesh" (Gen 2:18-23). There is a reciprocity and compatibility between man and woman: they are made for one another, and together they somehow reflect the image of God. This congruity spills out into the whole of creation. Together, men and women are the stewards of the fish in the sea, the birds of heaven, and all living creatures that move on the earth (Gen 1:28). With the completion of God's creative work, man and woman stand together as the divine viceroy and proxy. In their relationship with the Lord, they capture and sum up the glory and splendour of all that exists. And then the serpent turns up.

With sin comes fragmentation, mistrust, blame, and banishment. The serpent tempts the woman by undermining her trust in God. "Did he really say you were not to eat from any of the trees?" it asks. "You will not die," it goes on, enticing her to taste the forbidden fruit (Gen 3:1-6). What the serpent is really suggesting is that God is not enough. Who wants to be a mere viceroy when, through having this product, by eating this piece of fruit, the woman can become a god herself? It's an early example of advertising. Notice too that it is the woman who gives the fruit to the man to eat – not the serpent this time. The serpent is far too wily a creature for that: it has realised that sex sells. With the original mistrust of God, with the desire to be self-sufficient, the whole balance of creation is affected. Woman and man, previously flesh of one flesh, now start covering themselves up, hiding themselves from one another and from God. I'm certain that the fig leaves mentioned in Scripture refer to more than simply a fear of nakedness. They represent a wholesale privatisation of human intimacy. The result of this relational breakdown becomes evident when the Lord calls to Adam, "Where are you?" Where once God looked upon his creation and saw in man and woman his own image and likeness, now he must search for them and seek them out. The fact that he bothers to do so demonstrates his infinite love for us. But the fragmentation continues. "It was the woman," blames the man, "It was the serpent," blames the woman; and suddenly they find themselves banished from the paradise God had given them.

We see in these texts of Genesis the reason for the power of our current day sex and shopping obsessions. We have begun to doubt that God is enough for us. We have begun to look elsewhere. And today, just as in former times, wealth, power, ambition, possessions, and possessive sex are all candidates to become that forbidden piece of fruit. If I own this object, or have this holiday, or earn this much, or get this posting, or sleep with her then I will be free; then I will be satisfied; then I will be a god. Like Adam and Eve, however, we are misguided and we are wrong. The only way to paradise, the only way to freedom, is by turning back to the Lord.

It is within this theological framework that I feel the call to celibacy can have some meaning. But celibacy must take its place within a whole package. If sex is replaced by greed or ambition or conceit then we are still no further on from Adam's sin. It is significant that the evangelical virtues always place celibacy (or, strictly speaking, chastity) alongside poverty and obedience. If I am free from the prevailing atmosphere of "must have" and "must be" then I am indeed a sign of contradiction. If I aim for celibacy in its widest implications then I will come across as someone for whom God is God: someone who has given up on substitutes because he has learnt that they can never ultimately satisfy his eternal longings.

The creation accounts give us another insight into our sexual natures. Men and women are reciprocal. We are made for one another. Through our sexuality and through sexual intimacy we complete one another. "This is why a man leaves his father and mother and becomes attached to his wife, and they become one flesh" (Gen 2:24). Together we are a unity – but there is more to it even than this. God has blessed our complementarity and said, "Be fruitful, multiply" (Gen 1:28). United, then, we are to be procreative. A theology of celibacy must find its place within this ideal of the sexual union of man and woman. Teachings on the celibate life that are based on ideas of ritual purity, or on some sort of denigration of sexual intercourse, have no place in our overall understanding of sexuality. I remember once, as a seminarian, being quite shocked by another student's attitude. We were congregating outside of St Chad's in Birmingham awaiting the start of the Chrism Mass for that year. Opposite the Cathedral is quite a posh hotel – I think it is called the Nelson. One of the students noticed a young man and woman, draped together in dressing gowns, peering through their curtains out onto the street below, watching us. He made some remark to the effect of, "Typical, having sordid sex when they should be attending Mass." I was shocked on two counts. Firstly, why should sex have to be sordid? Secondly, assuming they were married – and there was nothing to suggest they were or weren't

– why shouldn't they be having sex? The comment to my mind betrayed an all too familiar clerical prejudice: the world would generally be a better place if everyone was stuck in a Basilica somewhere, feeling guilty about their bedroom behaviour, and praying for forgiveness. A healthy celibate lifestyle should rejoice in the conjugal relationships of others. Indeed, by denying ourselves the opportunity for such intimacy and sexual intercourse, we are precisely upholding their value to a world that itself can be rather disparaging about sex and marriage.

The ideal relationship of Adam and Eve as presented in Genesis, however, comes before the Fall. When we read on, and take into account the full effects of that first sin, we find the ideal tarnished somewhat. Read about the rivalry of Eve's first two children, Cain and Abel (Gen 4:1-16). Read about the difficulties of Abram and his barren wife Sarai, and her jealousy over Hagar the slave-girl (Gen 16:1-16). Relish the sexual treachery and politics in the stories of Jael's tent-peg (Judg 4:17-22), and Samson and Delilah (Judg 16:4-21). Recoil at the brutal practicality of the tale of the rape of the daughters of Shiloh (Judg 21:15-25). Perhaps the story of King David is the most famous – and also the clearest – example of the distortion of sexuality through sin (Cf. 2 Sam 11:2-27). These pages of Scripture merely reinforce our own experience. We have in our own times: sibling rivalries, inequality against women, homosexuality, marital breakdown, domestic violence, sordid affairs, rape, and child abuse. We play emotional games, and lie to one another, and have sex with ourselves, and manipulate conjugal rights – sometimes all within a "happy marriage." It is a simplistic and an inaccurate theology which argues that homosexuality, bisexuality, sexual perversions and addictions are all symptoms of fallen man, whereas heterosexuality has somehow escaped unscathed. The truth is that the whole of sexuality is fallen and seeks redemption, along with every other facet of our human nature.

It is, then, within the process of redeeming sexuality that

celibacy takes its proper place – alongside Christian marriage. Not that sexuality is bad and fallen, and that therefore sexual abstinence is the only answer (with Augustine's proviso of marriage as the remedy for concupiscence). Rather the opposite: by a celibate lifestyle which is generous and loving and affectionate and lived "for others" we demonstrate the true meaning of sexuality – the instrument through which we love others, not merely as commodities, not merely for the pleasure or comfort or support they give us, but simply because they are "other." As celibates we have the opportunity to manifest the self-giving love of God himself. And this celibate sign must be offered to the world alongside the sign of sexual intimacy in Christian marriage – the corresponding sign of God's creative love which holds us together in unity.

What, then, of those "grey" areas of sexuality? What place does any form of sexual longing have that deviates from the ideal proffered in Genesis? How can the homosexual or confused bisexual find a place for him or herself in the restored paradise of Eden? I suppose here it is helpful to remember that the redemptive work of Christ is not merely restorative but is indeed re-creative. John's apocalyptic revelation was of a "new heaven and a new earth" wherein the voice of the One sitting on the throne spoke, "Look, I am making the whole of creation new" (Rev 21: 1-5). In many respects a Christian struggling with a homosexual orientation is little different from a Christian struggling with a heterosexual orientation: both are called to live generously and with honesty. People may get hot about the collar over homogenital acts but then turn a blind eye to some of the selfish, self-serving, and self-loving things we do in the name of heterosexuality. We all need to be saved; we are all offered a place in Christ's re-creation. We see the model of our redemption in Christ's death and resurrection. Some of the early Fathers of the Church drew a parallel between the cross and the Tree of Life referred to in Gen 3:22-23. The cross is, of course, practically speaking, a complete perversion of that tree. Whereas in Genesis the fruit of the tree bestowed immortality, the cross was merely a tool of Roman execution. Jesus, however, doesn't "magic" the crucifixion away. He doesn't side-step its horror, but rather he meets his death head on, he embraces it. In so doing, he takes up the perversion and shamefulness of crucifixion and transforms it into the means of eternal life. Going back to the Church Fathers' terminology, Jesus doesn't merely restore the cross to be the tree of immortality; he ensures that it becomes the tree of eternal life. In the act of redemption, Christ doesn't restore or replace a paradise perverted and lost through sin with a replica, but in fact makes the fallen world the vehicle for something new and even greater: the kingdom of heaven. This model of redemption then can be applied to our sexuality – whether we are heterosexual or homosexual or whatever. Through sin our sexuality has in different ways, and to different degrees, become a perversion of what it was meant to be. Through redemption our fallen humanity becomes the vehicle in which we encounter the divine and allow ourselves to be divinized. So the redemption of a homosexual doesn't consist in their undergoing revulsion-therapy until somehow they become straight. It exists in their making use of their homosexual inclinations – their way of relating and loving – for God. It means allowing the Holy Spirit to work through their sexuality, filling what is fallen with grace and divine presence. The same is true for the heterosexual. The challenge of the cross is to allow Christ to transfigure and make use of a sexuality that has hitherto been somewhat turned in on itself through sin. A new vision, a new way of dealing with our sexual natures is being offered in this Christian theology. With redemption, the gifts we have been given by God (our sexuality among them), although affected by sin and concupiscence, can now become themselves the vehicles for God's kingdom of love and peace.

Here again celibacy fits into the picture. By renouncing genital sexual behaviour the celibate says quite clearly to society that sexuality is more than mere sex acts. He or she shows the world that the most important aspect of sexuality is not gratification but relationship. Furthermore, a celibate who has voluntarily given up the possibility of sexual intimacy stands for all who do not have such a choice. Someone who freely chooses to forego genital behaviour and is still seen to live a happy, fulfilled and love-filled life is a palpable reminder to the world that we are more than who we sleep with. I was struck very early on in my priestly ministry by this power of celibate living when I was called to give a talk to some patients in a local psychiatric hospital. I had prepared some long-winded waffle on the pastoral care of the sick but, when I got there, I realised they were expecting an "any questions" session. So I had to play it by ear. It was when they realised that I was celibate that I most aroused their interest. All of them were single, largely in virtue of being sectioned on a male only ward in a long-term institution. Many of them, I suspect, would have been incapable of sustaining any permanent intimate relationships. To them, I was a young man freely embracing a sexual lifestyle that they found themselves stuck with by imposition of circumstance. As we talked together about the celibate life, I sensed that their admiration of me grew and I actually found my own view of celibacy being bolstered by their appreciation and understanding. Here was I, by my free choice of celibacy, effectively saying to them, "It's okay to be single. You can be happy and fulfilled and normal." It made me think about other types of celibates: widows and widowers, the divorced and separated, those who remain single due to their sexual orientation and religious beliefs, those for whom the right person just never came along. None of these positions is necessarily involuntary or long term – indeed, there is nothing to stop a widow remarrying – but to all of them the charism of freely chosen celibacy reinforces their own innate dignity as sexual human beings. In a way, we're back to the concept of sex and shopping. Celibacy is a countersign, a flesh and blood reminder that we are more than mere sexual merchandise.

All of this may seem rather idealistic and, at times, far removed from our actual experience or feelings. I am grateful that I do have my lucid moments when this vision of celibacy is lived out. But I also must admit to sometimes feeling myself frustrated and caught up in a sexual straight jacket. Living any sort of an altruistic sex life is quite hard when beset with the temptation to masturbate, or manipulate. Being aware of my sign value to others can become quite a burden when I'm caught up in a vicious circle of sexual fantasy, or I'm falling head over heels in love, or I'm just plain lonely and in need of a little affection. Nevertheless, having some sort of theological framework in which to understand my sexuality and celibacy is still essential. I, at least, need to take courage from the bigger picture being offered; I, myself, need an ideal for which to strive.

At my ordination to the diaconate I made a promise to remain celibate for the sake of the kingdom, as a sign of my interior dedication to Christ, and in lifelong service to God and mankind. Pretty heady stuff. I can remember the moment before we were called to stand before the bishop. One of the ordinands with me started muttering to himself, "I've got to get out of here, I've got to get out of here." All around us friends and family watched intently as we traded in our biological posterity for service in the Church. I sometimes wonder what my family made of it all. I sometimes wonder what to make of it myself. Here am I, choosing to live a chaste and single life, so that I can be free to serve God and others. Am I mad, or simply an idealist? Why on earth should not being married and not having sex enable me to serve the Lord better? In what way does being celibate mean I am more equipped to deal with pastoral ministry? And yet this is the meaning of the solemn promise I took that day.

As the Catholic Church in England enters the third millennium, there are subtle changes taking place in people's comprehension of parochial ministry. With so many married former Anglican clergymen having been absorbed into dioceses around the country parishioners are quite rightly asking the question: so why do you have to be single then? I often joke that my view on the desirability of being allowed to marry depends upon my hormone levels at the time of asking. Similarly, with the number of sex scandals affecting the Church at the turn of this century, and with vocations dropping to a frighteningly low level, people are understandably looking around and questioning: who exactly is ministering to us, and who will be doing so in the future? Of course, scandals don't arise because we are celibate but because we are human, and flawed, and sinful. Marriage isn't going to change that; it'll simply add divorce and adultery to the list of our problems. Similarly, there is no evidence of any young army of prospective priests lining up for ordination, just waiting for the celibacy rule to be relaxed. Look in our churches – there is a major dearth of young people attending Mass in this country and priestly celibacy is the least of their reasons for non-attendance.

I suppose the minimum that can be said of celibacy is that it means we priests are a cheaper and more flexible work force. Most dioceses don't organise proper salary schemes, they accommodate their parish priests and assistant priests in the same house, and they move us around like pieces on a chess-board. If we were married we would need sufficient income to provide for our families; we would start to have separate houses – probably away from the church site itself – in order to bring up our children; and we would need stronger rights of incumbency to ensure our children receive stability and a decent education. It's not impossible – the Anglican Church has managed it; but it would affect people's perception of our ministry.

Is there a place, then, for celibacy within the diocesan clergy? What is the link between being celibate and being an effective minister? I believe that it boils down to the first part of the promise that we make at ordination: I am resolved to remain celibate as a sign of my interior dedication to Christ. It's not that I am necessarily any more dedicated to Christ than a married person. But, in choosing celibacy for the sake of the kingdom, I am trying to give a clear signal to those around me that Christ is the ultimate answer to all our longings. By being prepared to give up something that strikes at the core of my human nature, I am demonstrating that for all of us – married or celibate – Christ has the prior claim. And it is a signal that people understand. They may not really grasp the intricate detail of sacramental, sacrificial and sexual theology; but they do sit up and take notice. Here is someone mad enough to give up sex, to give up intimacy, to give up the chance to have children all for an ideal: Christ the Lord. If I'm sometimes wondering why I do it, then I can be sure those around me must wonder. It is a sign that works.

Celibacy affects our ministry in other ways too. Because I am free from the demands and pressures of being a husband and a father, I am potentially more available for those in my pastoral care. I can cancel, say, a trip to the supermarket in order to respond to a sick call because at the end of the day only I will starve. But if I have a family, if I have four young and hungry children to think about, then I can't. Similarly, I don't suffer the stress and time consuming worry of my children falling ill, my children bunking school, my wife becoming tired and worn down and feeling unloved, my marriage breaking up, and so on. In a world where myself and my family and my parochial ministry are all somehow vying for my attention and my time, clearly if I remove the family factor then I can make more time for ministry. However, the reality is also that I can make more time for myself. There is a danger – and I see in it myself – that over the years, and bit by bit, we twist celibacy for the sake of the kingdom into celibacy for the sake of ourselves. We become guarded of our space, and our time, and our possessions. We live a professional generosity, a ministerial competence, but no longer a lifelong (and should I add, life-wide?) service to God and mankind.

For celibacy to be a sign of anything to anyone it must be a life lived in love. People aren't impressed by just another bachelor but they are intrigued by encountering warm, loving, individuals whose lives are marked by service. The advice of Luke 6:38 is apt: "Give, and there will be gifts for you." Perhaps generosity can be the hallmark of authentic celibate living: generosity with our time, our gifts, our possessions, our love, in fact the whole of our lives. Maybe this is the way out of the sexual straight jacket I referred to earlier. Living for others we find ourselves; expending our energy outwards, channelling our love and affection to others in a manner appropriate to our calling, we simply have less time, less energy, less affection to lavish inappropriately on ourselves.

We are, of course, called to a type of intimacy. This is something that people seem to forget at times. Celibate priests need to be loved as much as anyone else. We need human company, we need personal friends, we need a certain amount of affection and understanding and tolerance. Treating us like asexual robots which never switch off is inhuman. I am very lucky to have a close family whom I see quite regularly. I am lucky to have this ready-made environment where I can relax and be myself and be loved. Others find a haven in solid friendships; some place to be ministered to by the affection and warmth of others. Such a refuge is essential if we are to keep our sanity and our humanity.

The celibate life can be a lonely one at times. We probably all have our pressure points where we cope less well with aloneness. For me, locking up after the last parishioner has left at the end of the Easter Vigil – or after Midnight Mass – is a poignant reminder that I am by myself. Having experienced the adrenaline rush of leading people in worship, having joined with them in the joy of the occasion, and having watched them and their families go out into the night, I stand alone at the door. Similarly, I feel acutely lonely on my return from a sick call in the middle of the night. I am tired, and stressed, and maybe emotional. I have just spent the last couple of hours dealing with a family in distress, and now I return to my empty bed. No one is there to ask me how it went; no one is there to ask me how I feel; no one is there to offer me the warmth and love and affection that I probably need right at that moment.

Perhaps the most important consideration to come out of such reflections on celibacy and sexuality is that all of this – the sexuality that I experience, the promise of celibacy which I have embraced, the community in which I live and which I serve as a priest, the support I receive from friends and family – all of this is the *locus* in which I will learn to love; it is the arena in which, together with Christ, I will work out my salvation. One of the beguiling facts of sexual fantasy is that it is pure fantasy and not the real world. It is an attempted escape from the real, concrete challenge to love those around me. Equally, the temptation to sexual encounter: unless I really am planning to go back on my promise of celibacy, I am merely playing a game. I can get involved for a while; I can say, "I love you" now and again; but, at the end of the day, it is all really a sham. I am seeking gratification – maybe genital, maybe affective – but I am not loving. I am taking, with little commitment to give. Again, I am running away from the real challenge to love.

I said towards the beginning of this chapter that I am a failed celibate. I have indeed failed at all sorts of levels; but I am not despondent. I believe there is a place in the Church – and in the world – for the witness to celibate loving. I have embraced, or rather am trying to embrace, that vocation, that life of witness. I believe that gradually, little by little, Christ will teach me how to love sincerely and honestly. In my failure I know I have to tie in all sorts of other factors: loneliness, stress, the need for human warmth, the desire to have children, the need to be loved uniquely by another, routine, boredom, the pressures of advertising, the influence of television, the internet, books, other people, frustrations in ministry, hormones, and so on; most of all the need to pray. I know there is a bigger picture, and that I am only dealing with a part of the jigsaw of my overall calling to holiness. But my experience of celibacy reminds me that I can't do everything by myself. It reminds me of the answer that the Lord gave to St Paul: "My grace is enough for you" (2 Cor 12:9). And for it all – good and bad – I am deeply grateful.

CARICATURES

"SO ARE you a Fr McNasty or a Fr O'Nice?" asked a cheeky sixth former, shortly after I'd been appointed the school's chaplain. "Will you be playing good cop or bad cop while you're here?" It's funny – and can be quite refreshing – how other people see us. Sometimes it can burst the bubble of our own self-importance. I remember the first pantomime in that same school: one of the students sent up the role of chaplain by wearing trendy jeans and trainers while keeping the dog-collar and smoking a pipe. He talked in a sort of stilted, "cool" language. "Hey, those crazy kids!" became his catch phrase. I'm glad to say I've never smoked a pipe, never worn clerics with jeans, nor used such a stupid phrase; but I recognised myself. How many times have I tried to be "one of the lads" and failed abysmally? It makes me think: the almost cult like success of the comedy show, "Father Ted", is not only to do with the quality of the surreal writing and acting, but also because it lampoons the ridiculousness of the clerical lifestyle itself – a lifestyle that purports to be so serious. Our lives as priests are, even to most Catholics, so unusual (and sometimes our behaviour so bizarre or misunderstood) that we can be parodied all too easily.

We are not all the same, of course. There are as many different types of priest as there are different and unique individuals called to priesthood. Indeed some of us are more of a "character" than others. Nevertheless, we do share similar traits and it's not that uncharitable to suggest certain stereotypes. It is interesting, too, that the caricatures to be drawn of the clergy – and the labels we give them – can differ widely depending on who is doing the drawing. One parishioner's Fr Sensitive is often another person's Canon Two-faced. It is all to do with perspective. I think there is a value in looking at some of these caricatures, or stereotypes, because they can actually tell us something. Initially they indicate how we priests are perceived by others. To many outside the Church we are simply a weird or a wonderful (depending on the point of view) bunch of misfits. They tell us how patient people can be at times – and sadly how hoodwinked – despite some of our antics. They tell us, also, about how we see ourselves – for we too, the insiders, have our caricatures of one another. Most of all they remind us of our humanity. Although the characters I am about to portray are indeed exaggerated, they have their basis in tendencies that, if we are honest, can surely be found in one or other of us.

Perhaps the most easily identified type of priest is the curate breaker. This is the old school parish priest whose role is to stamp out the college-boy radicalism and idealism of his juniors; to mould, and shape, and make a man of his assistants. He has usually been in charge of the parish for twenty or more years, may well be a canon, and is almost certainly a monsignor. He probably has the ear of the bishop, too, and if ever a complaint was made we all know who would get moved. This is a man of vast pastoral experience and wisdom; a man who himself was probably "broken" as a curate, and – let's face it – it didn't do him any harm. His methods are a mix of dictatorial benevolence and plain old-fashioned tyranny. He operates a "one size fits all" model of priesthood, and that means trouble ahead for the curate full of his own ideas. "Such a priest doesn't exist these days," you protest. I can assure you he does. I know of a number of young priests who have had to put up with intolerable bullying, and some who have suffered nervous breakdowns as a result. I have heard first hand stories of good, committed men being treated like children: locked out of their own homes at night, unless they got back before the PP had gone to bed; not allowed into their own kitchens, in case they upset the housekeeper's milk rota; informed of their day's timetable at the breakfast table, with no consideration for the fact they might have made their own appointments; shouted at during Sunday lunch, simply because they dared to express an opinion; overruled or undermined in front of parishioners, not because they were wrong but just to remind them who was boss; given an impossible workload, and then scalded for being lazy when they failed to fulfil it. Our pastoral life is difficult enough at times without this sort of highhanded authoritarianism. Often the examples of cruelty seem small and rather petty when listed out of context. However, put them against the backdrop of a busy and demanding ministry, and bear in mind that they take place in the home of the young, and usually inexperienced, priest – in the very place where he should be able to relax and recover and find support from the day's pressures – and we have a sure recipe for unhappiness and growing resentment. It strikes me that this sort of behaviour is not only un-priestly, it is basically unchristian. And yet it goes on and is allowed to go on.

Although this "model" for easing curates into pastoral ministry is largely dying out, there do exist more subtle forms of curate breaking. I've watched a parish priest at a clergy social bark orders at his curates in a way most people wouldn't even talk to a dog. His assistants generously defend him as being a benign dictator – but he's a dictator all the same. I've been in presbyteries where you have the distinct impression that it is the parish priest's house, and that his curates are merely lodgers. This may be understandable – after all, the curates come and go whereas the PP has been there for years – but at the end of the day, it is the parish house: the home for all of them. Surely the more experienced priest could rise to the challenge of hospitality: to ensure that however long or short his assistants might be staying, they will feel fully at home. Sadly, there are numerous examples of breakdowns in communication: priests who live together, work together, but who correspond solely by means of notes left on the stairs; priests who are supposed to collaborate but effectively minister entirely separately of one another – the only point of contact being their Mass schedule. I have even heard one story (and I can't really believe it's true) where the relationship between parish priest and assistant has sunk to such depths that they now have separate fridges in the same kitchen, and refuse to make each other cups of tea. Psalm 133 becomes all the more poignant: "How good, how delightful it is to live as brothers altogether." Of course these problems are not all dependant upon the parish priest. He may, indeed, be a gentle, kind and caring man lumbered with an idiosyncratic or even a bullying curate. The sad reality may be that the curate breaker is the curate himself.

I realise that I have been extremely lucky in the first few years of my priestly ministry. Appointed to a busy and in many ways quite a difficult parish, I have lived with two parish priests in my time and thank God for them. Both are ex-religious, coming from a more collegial and, in some ways, more democratic schooling than the usual diocesan set up. I think this shows through in their approach to living with other clergy: collaborative at every level, even down to the choosing of the newspaper. To my mind, this is how it should be. We are, by virtue of our ordination, co-workers with the bishop; we are, by episcopal appointment, co-workers entrusted with the spiritual and temporal up-building of the people of God within our parish. Our roles are clearly co-operative and our living is of necessity largely communal (Cf. Code of Canon Law, cc.5451 and 5502). The theology underpinning our relationship is to be essentially Trinitarian: lives poured out to one another in love and service; ministry and mission shared – together with the people of the parish – within a dynamic community. The curate breaker mould is actually rather monarchical: authority dispensed from on high, dished out begrudgingly and merely because of practicalities; all rather removed from the vision of Vatican II's intimate brotherhood of priests, called to mutual care for one another and for their people (Cf. *LG* 28). Working together is also just good sense. Life is so much easier in the long run if we make the effort to get along. There may be examples of personality clashes – I suppose that's inevitable – but then they should be acknowledged and addressed, not allowed to go on festering and undermining the work of the gospel. It's also a matter of integrity. Week-in and week-out we preach the forgiveness of sins, the call to be compassionate, the need to love our neighbour. How sad if we fail even to attempt to translate those homilies into some sort of concrete reality behind our presbytery doors.

All this can make for a humbling meditation, when I realise that sometimes I am not too far removed from the breaker's prejudice. How often am I unfairly critical of other priests who don't fit in with my model of ministry? The tendency to see the world purely on our own terms is quite insidious, even for those of us who think we are pretty enlightened. How many times have I secretly looked down my nose at the seminarian on summer placement in my parish? "He'll soon learn," I've thought to myself rather patronisingly, as if I was the only one with anything to offer in pastoral terms. How many cock-ups have we had with the parish diary, and all down to my incompetence? Effective communication takes thought and effort, and sometimes I just don't make the effort to think.

The next caricature might be called the visitor. This is the man whose primary pastoral concern is knocking on doors. Come four o'clock every weekday afternoon he's to be found muffling himself in scarf and donkey jacket, ready to trudge the streets. He is organised, systematic and committed. He has pre-planned his route, he visits every Catholic house in each street, and he doesn't let himself go home before nine. He probably plays a round of golf on his day off with other, like-minded visitors, during which they compare parish statistics and boast about how many families they "got through" last night.

Like the curate breaker, the visitor is a dying breed these days. In some ways this is quite sad. Visiting is certainly one of the best methods to get to know your parish. It's amazing how differently people relate to you once you've enjoyed a cup of their tea and munched your way through a few of their jaffa cakes. However the reality is that, with the current shortage of clergy and the increasing demands of a busy parish life, the visiting practices of old are often now impossible. There must also be the recognition that society itself has changed. In some areas it is no longer appropriate to descend upon a family around teatime. The idea that everything should come to a stand-still just because the priest has turned up may not be a part of people's expectations anymore. The days of front rooms and best china are definitely in decline. A number of times I've been left on the doorstep with the question, "So why are you here?" The answer, "To test your tea-making ability," is rather tempting, but I've never dared say it yet. One friend of mine – admittedly in a very well-heeled parish – found he couldn't even make it up the garden path when he called by on one parishioner unexpectedly, because of the security fencing and the electronic gates. He now visits by appointment, usually for dinner. There are amongst us, however, still a number of stalwarts left; a minority of clergy intent on visiting house after house. These were the type of men we were sent to as students – perhaps precisely to hone our visiting skills. "You should be able to get through twenty in a day," I was once advised, "so long as you don't spend more than ten minutes at each." I sometimes wonder if this isn't simply the clerical equivalent of battery hens: packing them in to keep the numbers high. It's certainly not my definition of visiting. Visiting is about letting yourself be received into the company of others; allowing them to welcome you with generosity and love; engaging with them as fellow human beings. Can this really be done in ten minutes? The danger exists, of course, of not visiting at all; of allowing these difficulties of time, of expectation, of purpose and practicality to become immutable objects strewn across our pastoral path. "I don't visit because I haven't enough time," or "because people don't want me to," or "because it's just not necessary" actually mean – for me at least – that I don't visit because it's too cold, I'm too tired, and I just can't face it at the moment. If we do give up visiting altogether, then in some ways we become simply another professional service, much like a lawyer or a doctor. Everything becomes appointment based and office bound. It would be a shame, I think, and somewhat removed from John Paul II's image of us as "artists" of pastoral work (Cf. *NIN* 6).

I suppose the challenge of the modern parish is to find new ways of getting to know the people. I know of one priest who still visits systematically but who limits it to one or two evenings a week. He may only visit four families in a day – he is trying to avoid the battery hen approach – but he is confident that eventually he will get around to everyone. Another approach is to plan our calls alongside our sacramental work. Trying to see the parents before a baptism; calling in on families of first holy communion and confirmation candidates; comforting bereaved relatives and helping them with their funeral arrangements; caring for the sick and house bound; blessing the houses of newly married couples (or, these days, instructing cohabitees for their impending marriage) – any one of these can be the opportunity to get out of the presbytery and into people's homes. It strikes me that there are ways and means of getting out and about – it's simply a matter of priorities.

The visitor – particularly in his more manic manifestations – can be but one example of quite a broad stereotype of cleric: the action man. This type of priest can be pretty inspiring at times: he may be the hospital chaplain always on call; he may be the counsellor constantly to hand; he may be the administrator getting things done. This is the priest who misses his days off, who doesn't eat lunch, and who hardly seems to sleep. His parish is often buzzing with activity and new ideas – social, pastoral, catechetical, and spiritual – and at the centre of it all is himself. This man's diary is heaving with appointments and his days are busier than busy. A less charitable word for him might be workaholic. Of course he despises shirkers: "Carpet slippers are the sign of a lazy priest," said my first PP, as I settled down in front of the telly one evening, my feet snug in a new pair my mum had just bought me. He was only getting his own back, as I'd been teasing him earlier about his action man antics. Thankfully he wasn't a fully-blown workaholic or else we might not have got along. Inspiring at times they might be, but they're also quite exhausting.

My worry about such action men is twofold. Firstly, their slavish addiction to activity raises the question: what are they avoiding? Such hustle and bustle throughout the day betrays a certain discomfort with oneself. Clearly there are occasions when the parish consumes every moment of our time – but these are not every day. Indeed, parochial ministry can be quite unrelenting and is no respecter of our own needs, but only if you allow it will it take up all your time. It's almost as if the workaholic can only find meaning to his life through his activity. Perhaps the story of Martha and Mary would make a useful meditation here (Lk 10:38-42). Secondly, the action man seems to think himself indispensable. He has his fingers in so many different pies, he has placed himself at the centre of so many varied plans – how then will he cope when retirement, or illness, or incapacity, or old age eventually demonstrate how expendable he really is?

The tendency to be the action man is something I am aware of in myself. Long ago the slippers were put to one side as I began to respond to the demands of pastoral ministry more deeply. Over the years, I seem to find myself becoming busier and busier. I suspect it boils down to an inability to say "no". It quite suits my vanity that I am asked to do this or that. It bolsters my pride that I am the one people want to see. I am sometimes just too much of a coward to let people down. The net result of all this is that I often take on too much – to the extent that things don't get done, or don't get done very well. Fortunately, I can say that I am not a natural workaholic. Far from finding my *raison d'être* in the ceaseless round of daily toil, I usually become slightly resentful about it all. "In the end, your innate laziness will probably be your saving grace," says a close friend of mine, and I rather hope she might be right.

Alongside the visitor, another possible type of action man may well be the guru. This character is merely an exaggeration of a tendency that can be found in all of us: the need to be wanted. The temptation is to substitute our normal, healthy longing to be loved with the desire to be someone's saviour. This status of guru is one that we usually approach by stealth. It all starts with the admirable motive of trying to do our best. A pastoral need arises, we aim to make sure we are there. Spiritual questions are raised, we strive to be the ones with the answers. We are available, we say "yes", we are patient, kind, compassionate and caring. We become good confessors, wise counsellors, and hard-hitting preachers – and how we work at it. Nevertheless slowly, imperceptibly a change can begin to take place. Whereas once we were undoubtedly only the instruments – the vehicle through which Christ touched and healed his people – soon we start to think of ourselves as the tune. Soon it is our advice, our counsel, our presence which is important and which makes the vital difference to any given situation. Unfortunately, not only do we begin to believe this ourselves, but also we promote this belief in others. The example of John the Baptist stands as a reproach to such thinking. "I am not the Christ; I am the one who has been sent to go in front of him," he says (Jn 3:28). St Augustine, in his sermon on John's Prologue, comments upon this role. The Baptist is merely the voice, says Augustine, whereas Christ is the Word. Take away the Word, he argues, and what use is the voice (Cf. Sermon 293, 3)? So too with our ministry. Ultimately it is not our gifts which will make the crucial difference, but Christ himself.

The guru may echo these sentiments, but his actions betray a very different story. He will most likely have a string of devotees who will see only him for confession and pastoral advice. He may well have a clutter of converts who will attend Mass only so long as he is in charge. He has probably introduced a catechetics programme, but only he will give the talks. He might attend the SVP, the prayer group and the UCM each week, but sooner or later he will begin to dominate all three. He will be popular and called upon and be seen by all who know him as a pastoral success. He will, quite without thinking, have built up the parish largely around his own character. When finally, however, he is asked to move on, the guru will find that he cannot let go. Far from rejoicing in the gifts of his successor, he may allow himself to get caught up in shameless self-promotion and barely concealed criticism. The real problem is that he has put himself in place of the Lord, often without even realising it. Far from setting people free, the guru has made them – and indeed himself – prisoners of his own ego.

A fertile pasture for the growth of such gurus is the field of youth ministry. This work calls for charismatic leaders, those with a natural ability to be able to communicate and stir up faith in young people. Here, first impressions do count and popularity is important. Humour, language – even clothes – can all be cultivated to capture a receptive audience. However, alongside this youthful receptivity is also often a tender vulnerability. Teenagers are emotionally and sexually unsure of themselves. How easy, then, for the charismatic leader to inadvertently become the guru: the prop on which the youngsters rely far too heavily. How tempting, too, for the leader not to do anything about this situation. Popularity once courted for the sake of the gospel can so easily become popularity for the sake of itself. In the end, the guru becomes as dependent upon his followers as they are upon him. In a way it is a sort of spiritual materialism. Rather than collecting possessions, the guru begins to collect people – their gratitude, their admiration, their need of him.

In my own ministry I have felt the pull of such a temptation many times. My own apostolate to young people, my work within the parish, even the time and effort invested in writing a book such as this – it can all so easily become self-serving. For me, at least, there are two antidotes against such a tendency which I find work pretty quickly and effectively. Firstly, to reflect with honesty and humility on my many pastoral failures. Secondly, to spend time in the company of my family and friends – the people who have seen me at my worst as well as my best; those who have no qualms – and thankfully no hesitation – in knocking me back down to earth.

In apparent contradistinction to these types of workaholic priest stands the escape artist – the sort of clerical version of an absentee landlord. This is the man who is never there. He is always on retreat, or at a conference, or in a meeting. He can quote the exact canon that deals in law with the provision of holiday time. He will be quick to point out that annual retreats don't count as vacation, and that it's only a matter of justice that days off missed in one week should be carried over to another. Usually he has several other jobs alongside being parish priest – some to do with local chaplaincies, perhaps he's a diocesan representative for something or other, maybe even a national or international role. All of these give him ample excuse for his unavailability. If you tackle him on his absence he will be genuinely hurt. "I work as hard as the next man," he'll say. "That conference in Rome was work you know. And my skiing holiday in Andorra was because I added my Easter break from last year together with my Christmas break from this year, extended with about four days owing from the summer…" and so on. Listening to him defend himself, you realise that he has become a cross between a calendar and an accountant.

In a lot of ways I suspect that the escape artist and the workaholic are actually very similar. Both seem to be indulging in a fair bit of avoidance. With the artist it would appear to be the parish that he is avoiding. Perhaps he doesn't feel entirely at home in parochial work. Maybe the pastoral demands are just getting too great. This tendency to eschew aspects of our ministry isn't reserved to the absentee landlord alone, however. The more pastorally adept we become as priests, the more skilful we are at foreseeing and forestalling potential problems. We have learnt to steer clear of the things we really don't like to do. The more advanced among us – which is often synonymous with the more senior – have the ability to delegate; in other words the faculty to dump on our curates. There are, of course, some rather obvious forms of avoidance. We spend time in retail therapy when we could be getting on with something more important. Comfort shopping is an aspect of the life of almost every priest I've ever met. It's probably tied in with celibacy in some way, and is certainly a result of the curious hours that we work – but it can also mean that we are bored because we're not really fulfilling our parish duties. A similar evasion is tying ourselves up in committees and meetings, or fiddling around on the computer producing newsletters and booklets. These may be time consuming chores, sometimes necessary, and almost always boring; but they're certainly easier than engaging with real people with real problems. For the fully-fledged escape artist, however, the problem is more than simply avoiding one or two aspects of ministry. Their whole life has become a game of circumvention. They are flitting – more often than not rather unhappily – from one thing to the next, from one job to the another, from this parish to that, trying to find their niche. Just like the workaholic, the artist is searching to find his *raison d'être*.

The next caricature is the misery guts priest: the Fr

McNasty to which my sixth former referred. For such a priest, everything is too much trouble. Ask him to baptise your baby and he'll grill you about your Mass attendance. Enquire about a wedding date and he'll moan on and on about how much people spend on flowers these days, and how correspondingly little they donate to the Church. If you want to start a new initiative in the parish – say a prayer group or a bible study – the answer will be "no." "The hall is booked on Tuesdays," he'll growl, "and you can't come into the house." His whole ministry has become a sort of lifelong complaint: people don't do enough, they expect too much, and he doesn't see why it's his job. This state of affairs may well have come about because of the demands placed on him over time. Bit by bit he has been pecked to pieces with pastoral problem upon pastoral problem. He was probably quite generous and open-minded when he started out, but gradually such liberality has ebbed away. With each passing year he has grown more tired and felt less appreciated. He may still be a hard working priest, but now, sadly, there is something slightly begrudging about it all. This stereotype would seem to call for an older, more experienced man. However, there is a young McNasty too. The young misery guts is a quick learner. He has adopted all the attributes described above in half the normal time. He is on a sort of accelerated promotion scheme when it comes to being miserable. I often wonder with these characters exactly when the generosity was squeezed out of them. Maybe the seminary was to blame. Perhaps they've always been somewhat melancholic. Whereas parishioners are patient and sympathetic of older, tired priests, they have an understandably lower tolerance level towards young men with such a miserable attitude. Often they go unnoticed until they become parish priests themselves – simply because up until that time they have not had the opportunity to say "no" at levels which affect quite so many people. Sometimes such negativity might be a symptom of someone just not coping. Even as assistant priests we are pretty much unsupervised and left to sink or swim. It could be that a moaning curate is nothing more than an unhappy curate – someone who needs a bit of support and help with the difficult demands of pastoral ministry. Sometimes being a misery is purely part of churchmanship. If a young priest tends towards the young fogey model then his lack of generosity may be down to his overall distrust of the modern world. Vatican II was a mistake, he thinks to himself, as he harangues relatives over their inappropriate choice of music for their father's funeral. Saying "no" and hiding behind restrictive rubrics is merely a way of keeping things at bay – I suppose a rather weak attempt to bolt a stable door some thirty or so years too late.

It's quite easy to be critical of such ungenerous characters, but as always we can see something of ourselves in them. My patience and understanding have been sorely tested over five years in a busy parish, and I have begun to realise just how miserable I can be at times. The occasions I catch myself saying, "Oh, what is it now?" whenever the doorbell goes or the telephone rings is gradually increasing. The list of woes which I whinge about with fellow clergy seems to be getting ever longer. I have given stiffer penances in confession on a Saturday morning, just because I was tired or fed up. I have rattled through my third Mass on a Sunday in order to get to my lunch or watch something on the telly. I have snapped at people, moaned about them, and refused to listen. I have even been downright rude now and again. Fortunately, all of this is outweighed by the reaction of my parishioners. I suppose they've known me long enough now to recognise my mood swings, to spot when I'm likely to be tired and not at my best. More often than not I find myself humbled when my tetchiness is met with nothing but understanding and love. I suppose it is acceptable to have "off days" – we are only human after all – but when our priestly lives begin to become one long "off day" perhaps something needs to be addressed.

The final stereotype I want to examine is the cleric. The

first image that springs to mind is of the smartly attired clergyman: all sharp black suits and shiny black shoes – or cassocks and cummerbunds; all collars and cufflinks. This is the man who will have every conceivable clerical outfit for every imaginable ecclesial occasion. His room will most probably be dripping in lacy antimacassars and doily-like table mats. His shelves will be stacked high with dusty and unread theological tomes from the 1930s and 40s. His walls will be cluttered with pictures of churches, especially Roman churches, and somewhere – I guarantee it – there will be a framed photograph of his audience with the Pope. This man may be either young or old – his personal library has no bearing on his age or his time of theological training; it is more akin to the back room of a local second hand book shop, housing the discarded and discounted of yesteryear.

In fact this caricature is slightly misleading. All that has been described could indeed be an example of clericalism – and more often than not it is – but it isn't necessarily so. It could equally be an example of poor taste in interior decor, or simply of someone who likes dressing up. The real cleric is just as likely to be a trendy priest in jeans and polo shirt, or a Fr Liberal, with shelves stuffed full of well-thumbed commentaries on Vatican II. Clericalism cuts across every boundary. It can affect the curate breaker and the broken curate, the visitor and the absentee, the guru and the misery. The one characteristic that will unite them all is an over-blown sense of being set apart. Clericalism is a mind-set by which we, either consciously or subconsciously, believe ourselves to be of a higher caste than those around us. It is the practice of definition through differentiation. We use our dog-collars to get preferential treatment. We give one another silly titles in order to make ourselves feel slightly more important. We cultivate an air of trustworthiness and learning so that people will believe the most ridiculous and unlearned things we say. We protest and grimace at the pedestals laid out for us, and then happily take our places, head and shoulders above the crowd. We refer to the dignity of our priesthood, conveniently forgetting the priesthood of all the baptised. Clericalism, at its worst, is a cult of status.

Indeed we are set apart: we are radically altered through our ordination. However, we are set apart for a new relationship with those around us, not set apart for our own sake. As John Paul II wrote in *Pastores Dabo Vobis*, we priests exist in order to proclaim the gospel to the world and to build up the Church. We do not exist purely to be some sort of separate model of other worldliness. We are to be men of communion, of mission, and of dialogue, he argues. How can we possibly fulfil such a vision if we spend most of our time hiding behind a clerical identity? If we are overly busy setting ourselves apart and engaged in acts of differentiation, at what level will we be able to dialogue and commune with our people? We will simply turn ourselves into some sort of bizarre irrelevance – either through our archaic dress code, or our authoritarian manner, or simply by our being aloof (Cf. *PO* 3).

There are numerous other caricatures I could have portrayed in this chapter which would equally provide for entertaining meditation. I have chosen these particular ones because they are exaggerations of tendencies I see most clearly in myself. Even the apparent opposites – the action man and the escape artist – raise questions as to how I conduct my ministry. You may feel I have exaggerated them too far, but it is the temperament behind them that is important. Do I tend to be prejudiced, to be cruel, as in the curate breaker? Do I tend to be flighty, uncommitted, as with the absentee landlord? Am I engaged in a serious attempt to get to know my people, or merely playing a numbers game, or perhaps not bothering at all (the visitor)? Is my essential priestly identity caught up with Christ, or caught up with self (guru and misery guts), or activity (workaholic), or status (cleric)? The problem with all of these dispositions is that they restrict and minimise our role as priests. Their common effect is to distort our relationship with God and with one another. Their remedy lies in an honest appreciation of – and reflection upon – our daily lives, and a continual attempt at a renewal of our priestly service. As *Presbyterorum Ordinis* says, we will find holiness in our own distinctive way precisely in the sincere and tireless function of our priestly office (*PO* 13). In other words, the challenge of our vocation is to grow beyond such tendencies by the exercise of a generous ministry, and so to become not mere caricatures, but real people.

SIMPLICITY

SIMPLICITY was a resolution I made two years ago at the end of an Ignatian retreat. I had spent the past eight days in Penmaenmawr in North Wales. I was now going to return to my parish on the Norfolk coast and live differently. It didn't happen, of course. What did happen was that I went home, chucked out a few old clothes that no longer fitted and gave away a couple of CDs that I no longer listened to anymore. I toyed, too, with the idea of setting up a covenant with CAFOD, but didn't actually do it. I felt marginally guilty, for a while, about the size of my car. And then I got on with my life exactly as before. Maybe the one thing that did change – to some extent at least – was the content of my personal prayer. Simplicity became a sort of *basso continuo* to whatever else was weighing on my mind. It became a kind of nagging sub-theme demanding attention. If any-thing has been articulated in my prayer of recent years it would seem to be this one word: simplicity.

As I write this chapter I am reminded that my favourite gospel text has always been the story of the rich young man (Mk 10:17-22). Fourteen years ago, when I was just eight-een and trying to discern my vocation, it was this text that really spoke to me. Of course I could follow Christ in many walks of life. Undoubtedly I could be his disciple as well as a teacher, or a lawyer, or a radio DJ, or an actor, or any of the other jobs and professions I wanted to have at some stage. But in this text I heard a voice calling me to some-thing else: something more radical, something – for me at least – more challenging. "Go and sell what you own and give the money to the poor, and you will have treasure in heaven; then come, follow me." It is a text that still frightens me because I realise that I have singularly failed to respond to it. When I look at my life, it seems to me as if I am collecting ever more material possessions. I am growing increasingly comfortable and correspondingly becoming less bothered about the radical nature of my existence. What, I wonder, are the riches to which I am still clinging? Why am I unable to let go of them, unable to give to the poor and follow the Lord? It is true that I am a most unlikely ascetic. I suffer from a bad back and so straw mattresses on cold stone floors are out, I'm afraid. I was once advised by a priest in confession to stop fasting during Lent as it was only serving to make me even more irritable and depressed than I can be at the best of times; so bread and water are a no-go too. I'm hopeless at getting up in the mornings – even when I go to bed really early – so hours of meditative prayer before dawn would look pretty improbable as well. And yet, time and again in prayer, the message would seem to be this: that simplicity is the key to my conversion, my priesthood, and my life.

One or two of my friends say I'm too much of a puritan. Even my brother once remarked with surprise at the fact that I had electric front windows on my car. "I'd have thought you'd have had the windows welded into place," he'd said, trying to be funny. "Surely a window that opens is a bit of a luxury?" All this despite the fact that my life is anything but puritanical. I suppose it's because I mope about some days feeling guilty and because I'm unduly critical of their possessions and their lifestyles (a perverse sort of jealousy in fact). One thing that came out clearly from that retreat in Penmaenmawr was that simplicity demanded generosity. The evangelical counsel of poverty is to be anything but a miserly kind of existence. It is not a call to some sort of dour, penny-pinching stringency. Rather, it is the invitation to use all of our resources (and not merely our possessions) for others. So, for me, simplicity means an end to my puritanical harping on about other people's wealth or extravagance. It means, too, an end to the moping guilt at what I do have and a new beginning to share with others my talents, my gifts, my time, in fact everything I am and possess.

Nevertheless, I do think that I am being challenged to look again at the material circumstances of my life. I haven't taken a vow of poverty, for sure, but I am attempting to live a life of discipleship. I profess to follow a Master who was an itinerant rabbi, who dealt predominantly with the poor and the outcast, who warned his followers that "foxes have holes" but that the son of man would have "nowhere to lay his head" (Mt 8:20). I claim allegiance to a Christ who asked his friends to take no purse or haversack, no spare tunic or sandals (Mt 10:9-10); to a Christ who proclaimed "blessed are the poor" (Cf. Lk 6:20) and who let it be known that it was "easier for a camel to pass through the eye of a needle than for someone rich to enter the kingdom of God" (Lk 18:25). Meanwhile I live happily in my consumer world worrying about the trendiness of my clothes or the decor of my house. I have a fridge full of food, I drive a decent car, and I take holidays abroad. It's all too easy to justify my cosy existence in the UK and conveniently forget that around the world people are dying of starvation or of disease due to lack of the most basic medicines; that people are caught up in wars not of their own making, are forced from their homelands, are naked and hungry and imprisoned and sick. It's all too easy to ignore, even on my own doorstep, the homeless and the helpless. I know all this and I feel bad about it sometimes, but I don't change my life. The Lord is saying to me, "Sell all you possess, give to the poor and come, follow me" and I act as if I only caught the last three words.

However, as I have already said, this call to simplicity is more than just a challenge to practice some sort of material asceticism. Rather, it is the opportunity to look again at the whole of my complicated life. The preceding chapters have examined my vocation to the priesthood, the importance of prayer, the demands of pastoral ministry, the structures in which I work, my life of celibacy, and the caricatures I choose to adopt to hide my real self. In all of this there is the perennial possibility of simplification, the ongoing call to live out a simple priesthood. In my personal life, how can I simplify my celibate loving and my relationships with friends and family? I think honesty is important here. I need to admit that I get it wrong at times, that I find it hard at times, that I need support sometimes. I need to admit that I do want to love and be loved. Above all, it's important that I admit that I am a warm-blooded, human being with sexual needs and not a plaster-cast saint. I mustn't allow celibacy to become some sort of shelter in which to take refuge from the real, but sometimes harsh, world of love. I am called to love and to loving relationships, and simplicity means that I don't start complicating things by playing games to grab attention, or manipulating emotions to make myself feel better, or lying (even to myself) about who I really am and what I really need.

In my pastoral life, how can I simplify my dealings with those I care for and work with? To start with, maybe that clerical pedestal needs to go. I am no holier, wiser, or in anyway better than anyone else in my parish. I am there merely to point to and help make present their holiness, their wisdom, and together with them to lead myself a better, more sincere life. Perhaps I can look again at my preaching and sacramental practice. Am I speaking the truth or busy peddling clichés? Am I celebrating Christ's presence in our midst, or promoting my own presence (and ego) in the community of the faithful? Again, in terms of relationships, simple honesty is necessary: to recognise that I am shy and a bit hopeless at fraternity, but nevertheless asked to give it a go; to acknowledge that in certain pastoral situations I am quite gifted, but in rather more I am unqualified and somewhat clueless; to accept that I, like everyone else, am wounded and in need of healing and healers, as well as knowing that, at times, I will be the healer of others' wounds.

Finally, how can I simplify my prayer? I am called to stand before God with my people on my heart. I need to take that vocation seriously: to be sufficiently tuned into the needs of my people so as to articulate them with Christ before the Father; to love the people I am called to serve and to be so involved in their day-to-day lives that when I do pray – however I pray – they will be unerringly in the forefront of my mind. I need to pray, too, with my whole heart – my whole being – and not just my intellect. Prayer is to be an expression of my love of God and of his creation; an outpouring before him, not only of contrition and supplication, but ultimately of adoration and praise. Of course, I am asked to pray for the forgiveness of sins even as I am aware, often painfully, of my own sins. I need to be honest, then, with my God, and humble before him. Above all, I am not to babble. To pray with love, with honesty, and with humility before God must always be my aim, because these are the ingredients of simple prayer. And only when I pray with simplicity will I begin to live with simplicity.

Part Two

CHASING THE RAINBOW

CHATTING with an old school friend recently, we got talking about what all our peers were doing these days. He is the news editor on a local paper, while another friend of ours is a police sergeant on the fast track to promotion. Still another is a surgeon, soon to become a consultant. One of us (at least) is now a teacher, and married and head of his department. One works for a television company, another for a housing trust. Without exception, all have been successful. Here am I, however, a curate in a poor parish in a deprived part of Norfolk. "Did I miss the boat?" I asked my friend. "Your problem," he said, "is that you were always too much the idealist." I suppose we were all told the story, when we were young, about the crock of gold at the rainbow's end. I always imagined it to be guarded by a particularly nasty leprechaun – just to ensure that the utopia it promised really did remain out of my reach. My friend – a non-believer – thinks that priesthood, however socially worthy, is ultimately just a chasing of that rainbow.

The one thing that has always inspired me – both during my time of priestly formation and now that I am involved in pastoral ministry – is the witness of other priests. I have been touched by their example. I have been healed through their ministry. I have encountered God anew in their celebration of the sacraments. What people sometimes seem to forget is that we priests need priests too. My first year of ordination was spent in further studies and I was still living in a seminary. Whereas I was warned that I would be itching to preside all the time at Mass and would get fed up with concelebration, I found quite the opposite. I appreciated – and appreciate still – the prayerful way in which my brother priests said Mass. I was fed from their insights upon the Scriptures, nourished by their homilies. I was encouraged by the prayerful example of men who had been ordained for five, fifteen, and twenty-five years; impressed by their priestly commitment, their evident love of God. If I am, as my friend suggests, a blatant idealist, then I am certainly not alone; and I have learnt that the people who inspire me the most are precisely such fellow chasers of rainbows.

In this section of *Simple Priesthood* I have invited three fellow priests, and a deacon who is about to be ordained priest, to write their own stories. I have asked these particular people because of the diversity of their ministry, because of the variety of their backgrounds, and because what unites them is their engagement in pastoral practice. Above all, however, I have asked these four people to contribute to this book because they are people who have inspired me in my own priestly life. Editing their contributions, I have noticed that at least part of what they have written is a chasing away of false idealism, of false visions of what people think priesthood is or should be. The rainbow they still strive towards is that sharing in the eternal priesthood of Christ. But they are also mature realists: people whose lives and ministries ground them in the everyday reality of the Word Incarnate.

I agree with my non-believing friend. Priesthood is a chasing of rainbows. But what he has forgotten is the more ancient story about that multicoloured miracle: nothing about crocks of gold and nasty little leprechauns; everything about our covenant with God and the promise of new life.

CONVERSION:
THE CALL WITHIN A CALLING

John Udris

Ordained sixteen years ago for the diocese of Northampton, John Udris is currently the parish priest of St Teresa's in Beaconsfield. He began his pastoral ministry with two curacies in Kettering and Corby which lasted a total of ten years. He was then given a sabbatical during which he studied at the Angelicum University in Rome and obtained a licence in spiritual theology. It was there that he was able to focus his work on St Thérèse of Lisieux and he has since published a book about her spirituality entitled, *Holy Daring*. John is also the vocations director for his diocese.

It has proved to be one of the most precious gifts of the last few years of my priesthood, and probably the nearest I've ever come to a spiritual experience. I was finishing a holy hour, closing with a familiar, favourite prayer – one that I must have prayed many hundreds of times. It's a prayer I first met in my mid-teens but which still features some twenty-five years later, still steering me, still stirring me; like a poem that says what you've always wanted to find words for. And, although it strikes me now as a bit pretentious, I even had it printed on my ordination card. I knew from the first that this was a prayer for me. And to date it has lost none of its power. You may know it:

Father, I abandon myself into your hands,
Do with me what you will.
Whatever you may do, I thank you.

I am ready for all, I accept all.
Let only your will be done in me and in all your creatures,
I wish no more than this, O Lord.
Into your hands I commend my soul,
I offer it to you with all the love of my heart.
For I love you, Lord, and so need to give myself,
To surrender myself into your hands
Without reserve and with boundless confidence
For you are my Father.

This prayer of abandonment of the soldier-turned-hermit, Charles de Foucauld, had struck a chord with me straight away. It was intimate, daring, and full of a desire with which I could identify. And I suppose, for an earnest teen-ager in the first flush of a hunch that God might be calling him to be a priest, it was heroically simple. I must have prayed it pretty much daily ever since. Sometimes eagerly, sometimes gingerly. Sometimes in gratitude, sometimes in the grip of uncertainty. Sometimes out of piety, sometimes out of sheer desperation. I have felt both at home in its hopes, and often light years away from its yearnings. At times I sleepwalk through its words, oblivious to the blank cheques I'm signing. At others the words sound so alien on my lips I feel like a fraud and say to myself, "Who on earth are you trying to kid?" Quite often I find myself qualifying each phrase with mental reservations or keeping my fingers crossed that I won't be taken too literally. But there are times too when, however much at odds with them my life may be, these words sum up perfectly what I want to say. Or at least what I want to want to say. They are nearer the knuckle than any other prayer I know.

This particular day I was drawing a fairly dry and un-eventful hour's meditation to a close as usual with this prayer when I became aware of something that I'd never noticed before. Suddenly three of its words stood out in bold relief. Three little words which, after years of saying them, I could only now see recurring in the prayer like a refrain, once right at the beginning, once in the middle, and once again at the end: "into your hands". Everything in me leapt to attention, like when someone calls out your name. I experienced the sparking of all kinds of connections. All kinds of bells began to ring. I began to wake up to how important these words had always been. I remembered the occasion, funnily enough around the same time I first came across this prayer, when I had stumbled over a young person praying with open hands. I had never seen anyone pray like that before. It struck me so forcefully that I wanted to try it myself. And to this day whenever I want to kick-start my prayer that simple gesture says it all: into your hands. Now I understood why, of all the offices in the prayer of the Church, Night Prayer has never lost its appeal. Not because it's the shortest, but because at the heart of it is the responsory, "into your hands" (which years ago as a starry-eyed seminarian I took the trouble to learn in Latin as if to make something more of it and give it some gravitas). It suddenly clicked why certain hymns, the lives of particular saints, as well as specific passages of Scripture have held a strong attraction through the years. And why other prayers of abandonment, like that of Saint Ignatius, remain among my favourites. Remarkably, as if to confirm all this, a few days later I picked up a book of poems in which I had left a slip of paper some years before. The refrain of the poem I had book-marked was, "into your hands".

All this is rather ironic because I'm a bit of a control freak. I like to keep a tight hold on the reins. Coping comes just a tad too easily. And whenever things threaten to slip out of my grasp I begin to panic. I remember vividly at junior school going in for my first swimming certificate thinking no one would notice if I kept one foot on the bottom of the pool. At college my friends chided me for the chain mail I seemed to walk around in. I still crave security almost at any cost. With this new insight it began to dawn on me that somewhere in this vicinity is my besetting sin and my biggest liability both as a Christian and as a priest. This is where the fault line lies.

And why "into your hands" is the prayer for me, at the same time spelling out the path of my conversion.

Conversion is the call within every calling and a touchstone of every true vocation. "Am I answering God's call?" and "Am I being converted?" are in some ways the same question. The greatest confirmation that I am where I should be is whether or not I am being challenged and changed. Priesthood is the particular way God is gradually prizing my fingers from the things to which I cling in order to entrust them to his providence. This insight has been an integrating influence. Now, whenever I need some leads in preparing for confession, I look for lack of trust: the often all too subtle ways I try to keep control of situations, and of people; the manufacturing of my life and ministry to such an extent that the Lord gets little of a look-in. My fallen nature prefers to keep things firmly in my own hands. And I'm all too aware of how, if I can't manage this in reality, I retreat to fabricate it in a fantasy world where I can have things on my own terms – at least for the time it takes for the mirage to disappear into the sand.

But all this begs a further question. Why I do I want to be in control? What makes clinging my first resort? What's going on there? Have you ever suspected that your sins were symptoms of something more insidious, something more deep-seated? Fear, I fancy, is the reason I want to keep things firmly in my own grasp. A fear that the best voices in our tradition tell us is always the great enemy of faith. So not only is "into your hands" a way of examining my conscience, seeing where I need to be converted, it is also the antidote, the penance, the actual route of my conversion – my own particular exodus. Those three words trace the contours of the turnaround Christ's teaching is continually on the lookout for in my life. Whenever I try to answer their invitation I'm taking a step away from fear and towards trust. And it seems priesthood is the particular path of migration God has marked out for me.

This fear is present when I'm facing situations in which

I feel out of my depth. Listening to a young woman who has just lost her baby. Attempting to lead an RE lesson with a group of emotionally and behaviourally disturbed teens. Called out in the early hours to be with someone who is in the throws of a nervous breakdown. Sitting with a family as they struggle to take in the news that their loved one will not recover consciousness. Sensing the moment approach when someone will give voice to a trauma from their childhood they have never spoken about before. Giving a day of recollection to my fellow clergy. Finding myself falling in love with someone, or they with me. Or just simply the relentless routine that leaves me lurching from one thing to the next without any real time to get ready. Situations where I feel ill equipped and inadequate, or caught unprepared and off balance. Times when "into your hands" is a pretty desperate plea. Times when trust, though it is wrenched from me, can be raw and most real. Etched on my memory is the roundabout in my first parish from which I had to turn off towards the home of a family who had just lost their son in a motorcycle accident. I went round and round it – I don't know how many times – before finally summoning up the courage to indicate and take that turn. I find myself regularly circling similar roundabouts. But I know the making of me as a person and as a priest waits at the end of those exit roads, though at times they are taken with more terror than trust.

I sense this fear when I'm preparing the Sunday homily. Preaching has never come naturally to me. I know which side of the pulpit I would rather be on. And although I've been giving sermons week-in week-out for more than fifteen years, it doesn't get any easier. More often than not I'm desperately seeking inspiration on a Saturday afternoon, wondering what on earth I'm going to say. From time to time I've thought perhaps I should be a monk and spare myself the pain of having to preach. But then I have a sneaking suspicion that this is perhaps precisely why God has called me to secular priesthood – to learn and relearn, week by week, that I have to keep trusting that he will provide. Not to mention it makes sure that I pray. Furthermore, it safeguards against a streak of stinginess in my nature. "Hoarded grain goes bad," said Dominic, the founder of the Order of Preachers. His wisdom points to preaching as an important element in my own continuing conversion.

My dad is a hardened hoarder. During my childhood he built two huts and a coal-bunker to store the stuff he bought each week at the second-hand auctions (and that was after the garage and the first coal-bunker were full). I'm afraid I'm a chip off the old block. Instead of building more bunkers I build more bookcases to surround myself with more books for the security their knowledge seems to promise. During a retreat recently I was given a passage of the gospel for that day's meditation. It was the scene by the Sea of Galilee where Christ cooks breakfast for his apostles after the resurrection. I duly imagined myself as one of the disciples being waited on by the Lord, only to discover that my immediate reaction to Christ's handing me the bread and the fish was to put it into my knapsack for later. Spotting this Jesus said, "John, eat it! Don't you think I will provide next time too?" I was found out. I'm always afraid that he won't provide. And anyway it's less painful to be always on the safe side. Moreover, it showed me that there can be an immediacy missing in my relationship with the Lord. There was the clear implication that I can allow that relationship to become a stale, stockpiling of provisions, rather than something that is freshly cooked and eaten each day. I confess there are times as a preacher when I bottle out of the (sometimes painful) prayer involved in preparing a sermon. Instead I take refuge in a box of homilies preached on previous occasions and, pulling one out, think that this will do. "Re-heated food," I call it. Some day I may dare to burn the contents of that box, even though I'm already panicking at the thought.

More recently I have noticed something that helps to chase this panic away. Something I'm only just beginning to discover the power of: gratitude. It's there in de Foucauld's prayer: "Whatever you may do I thank you." And I sense, more and more, that this is an important ingredient in ongoing conversion. Gratitude grounds us in reality. It underlines our utter dependence as creatures, our total poverty. "Thank you," is the constant refrain of those who are poor in spirit. Moreover, it is the vocabulary of those who are at least learning to trust. I'm coming to see how key a component thanksgiving is in releasing my grip on things and relinquishing control. Looking at Our Lord, we see him giving thanks when he hasn't yet seen the evidence that his prayer has been answered (Jn 11:42), even in the face of failure (Mt 11:25) and, finally, on the very night he was betrayed (Lk 22:17). Everyday in the Eucharist I publicly proclaim, "We do well, always and everywhere, to give [God] thanks." But I'm only beginning, and very tentatively, to say thank you when I don't know how things will work out, when I sense that something is beyond me, and even when failure is staring me in the face.

I am petrified of failure and yet it has in many ways been a faithful, if ruthless, friend. I recall perhaps the rockiest moment on the road to priesthood. It was almost too late. My ordination was just six months away and I couldn't hide my panic. I requested a psychological assessment. It was clear to the assessment team and to me that I was a bit of a mess. When it came to the final interview I was asked what I thought the next step was. All I could say was, "Surrender." I remember the psychologist saying to me, "But you can't surrender from a position of weakness." What she meant was that abandonment can be an escape too – and an evasion of responsibility. I don't think I convinced her that, in this case, "into your hands" wasn't a complete cop-out. Perhaps I didn't realise then that it could be: that abandonment might actually be an abrogation of the onus by which we co-operate with God's grace; that we can't let go of something until and unless we've first properly got hold of it; that things need to be faced and embraced before being finally handed over; that truly to surrender oneself there must first be a self to surrender. Nevertheless I sometimes wish I could recapture the raw exhilaration of those days when, for once in my life, I was uncertain. When I found that weakness could be friendly and failure actually do me a favour.

One of the consolations that I've experienced more and more of late is a profound love for my people. It is something that has overtaken me on occasions when I'm celebrating the sacraments with them. I was aware of it at last week's wedding. As I placed my hand over Andrew and Ruth's joined hands to pronounce them man and wife, I felt a surge of love and concern that wanted to reach into the future and remove the obstacles they would necessarily have to face. I felt something similar last Sunday at little Matthew's baptism, praying for his protection as he grows up "to face the world with all its trials and temptations." I sensed it yesterday as I anointed Kitty, who is near to death, and commended her into the arms of the Good Shepherd. Such feelings are a consolation for me as a priest because they are a confirmation of that priesthood. Somehow they're reassuring me that I'm in the right place. They are little examples of the fulfilment I feel when I'm entrusting others into His hands.

Other kinds of confirmation in this regard are the conspiracies of grace you find yourself caught up in, when there's an unmistakable and often overwhelming sense that things really are in His hands. Like the words you are given in a situation – in a homily, in spiritual direction, or in the confessional – and you just know you weren't responsible. Like the visit you make at just the right moment. Like your appointment to a parish whose patron saint you've just been studying and writing about. Such things invite us to take the hint that someone else's hands are at work and that they are trustworthy, even when the experience may be bitter and excruciating. I will never forget the privilege of accompanying a woman whose whole life seemed to be collapsing around her. Having experienced the breakdown of her own health, she then had to witness helplessly her child's psychological breakdown and finally her own marriage breakdown. And yet she came to me one day to say that through it all she had learnt to pray, "Lord, if you won't take this away, then make this a way." What she was praying for was that all this wouldn't be a waste; that, if God wouldn't take it away, he would somehow make sure to make it a way to truth, to love, to a more abundant life for her and for her family. Her prayer, of a piece with Christ's own in the garden of his agony, has inspired me ever since, especially when the hands into which I am asked to yield would seem to be hard and brutal, if not actually non-existent.

I recall a retreat I made years ago. The retreat master asked us to imagine our lives as like a chessboard made up of many squares, each representing an area of our lives. He posed the question, "How many of these squares have you given over to God?" He suggested that, even though we may have allowed him influence over the majority of them, there were most likely a few – maybe just one or two – that we were still holding back. Then came the bombshell: "These," he said, "are the squares in which God is really interested." I've never forgotten that. Perhaps that in itself is significant. What he meant was that, wherever I am withholding from God, somewhere there a crucial chapter in the story of my salvation still waits to be written. One of those specific passages of Scripture that has always unnerved me is the sacrifice of Isaac. Of all the squares God could have asked for, surely his only son was the one Abraham had every right to hold back from handing over? Surely he could have said, "Sorry, Lord, but there I draw the line." I can hear Abraham saying: `Yes, I could have. And yes, of course, I wanted to. But somehow I knew that if I had withheld him, I would have been withdrawing into my own world, settling for a world where I call the shots, where things are on my own terms. And I knew that then Isaac would not be safe; that he would be in my hands and no longer in God's. Trust is the only way that we stay in God's world, a world where he will provide, a world where all is grace."

What God explicitly commends Abraham for is not "withholding" (Gen 22:16), not keeping Isaac for himself. It's no accident that he named that place "The Lord will provide" (Gen 22:14). And his trust was what triggered that provision. The harrowing thing is that he hadn't taken out any insurance just in case. There was no safety net. No fall back position. His faith was a free fall into unseen hands – a trusting to the point of no return, like the aerial acrobat who risks each unsupported moment trusting that, at just the right time, the trapeze will meet his waiting hands. Elsewhere Scripture contrasts the beauty of this kind of believing with those who "draw back" (Heb 10: 38-39), as it were, from the brink, recoiling from the risk involved, holding back from such an outrageous investment. Abraham didn't. What makes him such a convincing father in faith is the sheer agony he must have gone through. He didn't have his fear surgically removed. Here is someone who was prepared to hand over the most precious thing in his life: to let go of the living evidence that God's promises to him were actually coming true.

In his abandonment prayer, Ignatius prays, "You have given all to me, now I return it." I have to say I choke on that bit; but it's something Abraham could say and really mean. He knew that the price of living on providence was living on a kind of precipice; that God's gifts can be received but not possessed. Or rather, that they are received in their entirety only when we are ready to return them. Perhaps we all learn this lesson most painfully in our relationships. Certainly, as I struggle to love as a celibate, I experience here another aspect of the call to be converted. I'm all too prone to want to try and possess those I love. Little wonder friends have complained that my photographs of them feel more like a stamp collection. I'm aware that here, as elsewhere, there's a tendency to practice taxidermy on God's gifts. Too readily I seem to fall into the trap of turning them into trophies. Although there are times I wish she wasn't right, the words of Edith Stein are deadly accurate: "Sooner or later the lust for conquest usually – no, always – ends in loss." We can only hold on to what we're prepared to hand over, even though, on a bad day, open handed can really feel like empty handed.

In the Song of Songs there is a scene where the lover is within her house eagerly awaiting her beloved. She sees him looking through the window and she gets up to let him in, only to find that he has fled. She leaves the house in order to pursue him, out in the streets, out in the cold, out in the night. She was hoping he would come in. She finds, however, that she must go out. There is something compelling in that story line, even though it stings. It's got something to do with the elusiveness of love that will not allow itself to be possessed, hoarded, suffocated in the stale air of self-interest. It draws you out of your lair. Priestly ministry constantly prizes me out – out of my comfort zones, out of myself. It will not allow me to stay put, it stretches me and takes me to places I would otherwise not go. Sometimes I think to myself, "Wouldn't it be wonderful to have a normal nine-to-five job? One where I would learn to do just one thing really well and where things were more or less predictable rather than this plate-spinning, precarious existence where you're meant to be an expert in everything, when in fact you feel an expert in nothing very much." Then, in my saner moments, I sense that this is part of the pain and privilege of priesthood. This way I can't succeed on my own – at least not for very long. This way I keep being cornered by the call to surrender things to His safe-keeping.

Lately, I'm trying not to be discouraged by the fear that, bit by bit, I'm learning to befriend. I'm beginning to see that without it trust would not be trust – at least not the kind worthy of the name: the evangelical kind. I mean to say a trust that doesn't preclude questions. After all, the gospel begins with a young girl's "How?" and ends with a young man's "Why?" We trust in the midst of the unsolved and the unanswered. For me this means refusing to hide away from the heavy clay of my humanity, with all its motley motivations and Machiavellian scheming to escape. I'm learning to come clean. And here too I feel another hand at work, whose attraction is no accident and whose influence I have felt on-and-off since I first visited her home town at the age of ten: the little saint of Lisieux. But now I begin to see why Thérèse is the saint for me. Her teaching is all about the "boundless confidence" of de Foucauld's prayer. And why is that? Because it was the conversion she herself had to undergo. A graphologist, examining her hand-writing, has found "A child's fears and a warrior's resolve." Her story underlines what should have been obvious from the paschal mystery: that trepidation and trust are not mutually exclusive; in fact quite the contrary.

Recently, at a weekend for those discerning a possible vocation to the priesthood, I recalled an incident from Thérèse's life. She describes how one day, during prayer, a particular phrase of the book she was reading "resounded sweetly in the ear of [her] soul." The actual phrase that leapt out of the page at her was "the science of Love." She recognised her own reflection in those few little words. This seemed to corroborate the discovery of a few days before – that her vocation was actually to be "Love." The little way leading to that Love was "trust and nothing but trust." We might say she had – after seven years in religious life and just a year before she died – tripped over her true vocation, the call within her calling. With a view to getting some clues at the start of a similar trail, I invited those present over the weekend to begin to be aware of whatever "resounds sweetly in the ear of [their] soul." Telling the story of my own little grace, I suggested that the most persuasive proof of any authentic call of God lies in the conversion it always calls forth. Conversion is the corner-stone of every calling. And it is always ultimately toward love. For conversion is what makes us capable of that communion which, as well as being the ecclesiological context of every vocation, is the life-task and eternal destiny of each one of us.

ASSESSING THE TASK AHEAD

Ian Dalgleish

Originally from East Kilbride in Glasgow, Ian is now a priest of the diocese of Wrexham in North Wales, having been ordained for four years. He is currently parish priest of St David's in Tywyn and St Mair's, in Machynlleth. Prior to his priestly formation he obtained a degree in sociology. This article was prompted by discussions within his diocese over the future of the pastoral situation facing the clergy. A longer version was first published in a Scottish journal called, "Open House."

THE HISTORICAL CONTEXT

In the hundred years or so between the Restoration of the Hierarchy, the First Vatican Council and the Second Vatican Council – roughly, between the 1860s and the 1960s – the corporate identity of Catholicism in the British Isles was distinctive and clear. The community itself was close-knit, the result of years of social disadvantage and suspicion and of an ecclesiology that emphasised the Church as an institution and a perfect society. It was composed overwhelmingly of industrial working-class families. A large proportion of both laity and clergy was Irish.

The freedoms won by Catholics in the nineteenth century brought an era of hectic building: churches, schools, parochial halls, and social clubs. Membership of the local Church, the parish, was membership of a social-religious ghetto: Catholics, ideally, married other Catholics, baptised their children as soon as possible after birth, and later sent

146

them to Catholic schools. Baptism, first holy communion, and confirmation were important social and religious events in the life of the ghetto and reinforced its cohesion. At weekends many Catholics socialised in the club, or played sports, or went dancing in the hall, again reinforcing the community's internal cohesion.

The Catholic mentality during this period was insular and defensive. CTS pamphlets and other literature of the time (e.g. Hart's Student's Christian Doctrine) were polemical and frequently triumphalistic in tone: Catholicism was the only plausible philosophy, while all other systems and outlooks – communism, humanism, secularism, and not least Protestantism – were "erroneous opinions." "Good Catholics" did not talk about gospel values or the kingdom of God but were versed in the simplified scholasticism of the penny catechism. The sacraments, especially the sacrifice of the Mass and confession; Our Lady; the authority and infallibility of the Pope; respect for the authority of the clergy; a variety of popular devotions to saints: these were the principal motifs around which popular Catholic belief were organised. The job of the priests was to maintain and service the ghetto, which they did by administering the sacraments, visiting homes, organising parish activities; and to uphold the Church's authority, which they did by preaching and by cultivating their own sacerdotal status.

SINCE VATICAN II

Despite its many attractions and achievements, this particular Catholicism was open to the charge that it was a self-contained folk religion which existed more or less independently of the gospel. The Second Vatican Council contained the promise of renewal and reform, but the promise was not fulfilled. The slogans associated with the Council, such as "openness to the world" and "the Church

147

as the people of God", the de-clericalising tendencies initiated by the Council and the movements for greater lay participation in the life of the Church, did not in fact lead to a new pastoral and missionary impetus, but became the justification for a process of embourgeoisement parallel to that of wider English society. Since the late 1960s the older lay-associations – the SVP, the Legion of Mary, and so on, which carried out different aspects of the church's apostolate – have steadily dwindled, while the new middle-class Catholics have preferred to occupy positions on the various committees, boards, and commissions that have proliferated, mainly under episcopal direction, during the postconciliar period. As Bruce Kent has noted, Vatican II was a phase rather than a new direction, and today "there is less genuine lay participation in Church affairs than there was in 1960 – though many more paid lay-professionals. There is certainly less sense of real mission than there was then."

The new middle-class Catholicism is far more accommodated to, and less critical of, the prevailing secular culture than the folk-Catholicism that preceded it. Its liberal variant is sceptical of tradition, of Church authority, and is generally (sometimes subtly) anticlerical. Typical middle-class causes are ecumenism, married priests, women priests, collaborative ministry, inclusive language: the sort of inward-looking, "churchy", often peripheral causes espoused by individuals whose material welfare is stable and secure. Middle-class Catholics look to the gospel for emotional well-being, for personal integration and meaning. There is a tendency to play down or disempower the social and economic content of Jesus' teaching: his directives about the dangers of money, wealth, and possessions are, in practice, seen as irrelevant or exaggerated. Middle-class spirituality is privatised, and finds expression in books, courses, and retreats that borrow heavily from the fields of psychology, therapy, and counselling.

The integrated or corporate character of pre-conciliar Catholicism has been succeeded by what is frequently called a "cafeteria" religion in which the consumerism of modern economic life has contaminated Catholics' religious attitudes and behaviour. This change is seen most clearly in attitudes about conditions for membership of the Church: weekly attendance at Mass (previously the definition of a "practising" Catholic), support for Church schools – areas where Church leaders would have expected lay people to show "loyalty" in the past. Wealthy Catholics who used to send their children to expensive Catholic public schools are tending now to abandon these in favour of more advantageous non-Catholic versions, their children's future career and prospects of advancement being considered more important than the so-called Catholic "ethos" of denominational schools. This can be seen in some ways as the logical (and successful) outcome of the efforts to create a Catholic bourgeoisie via prestige Catholic education.

Embourgeoisement is only one aspect of Catholic life since the end of Vatican II. During the same period the rate of lapsation, especially among the young, increased steeply, and the number of vocations to the priesthood and the religious life dropped, as the social and economic conditions which underpinned the ghetto disappeared and Catholics fell increasingly under the influence of the world outside its confines. One result of this is that, at the turn of the third millennium, there is in Britain a large pool of Catholics, from the age of forty downwards, who are extremely superficially Christianised – if at all; who have only a tentative connection with the life of the Church – or none at all; and who take their beliefs and values not from the Christian gospel but from contemporary culture – a culture dominated, via the media, advertising, and the entertainment industry by the ideological assumptions of the free market.

Ironically, but naturally enough – because changes take place gradually and most people do not alter their outlook on life overnight – any residual notion this generation has of Catholicism and the Church comes from the preconciliar ghetto and not from the modernising ideas that have characterised the thinking of Church committee elites since the 1970s. Many members of this generation still perceive the faith in traditional terms of obligation, of what is allowed and what forbidden, but in practice they choose for themselves what to think and do according to their own criteria. Certainly Catholic guilt (for example, for not going to Mass, or for otherwise not fulfilling obligations of Church law) is a thing of the past. Many bring their children to be baptised, and wish them to make their first communion and to be confirmed, but these occasions are seen as events of their individual family life, unconnected to membership of the local Church, or to a life of Christian faith and discipleship. Again, many couples wishing to have a Catholic wedding are already living together, and describe themselves as non-churchgoers. More and more often we see an approach to the faith which is that of consumer to provider of services: a request for a Church wedding, for their children's baptism, etc. is viewed as something akin to booking a venue for a birthday party or a disco. The suggestion that there should be spiritual and moral effort and involvement on their part – that the celebration of sacraments is meaningless outside the context of Christian faith, discipleship, and the spiritual fellowship of the Church – if often met with resentment and irritation.

The attitude of the clergy, as representatives of the institutional Church and as administrators of the sacraments, also still derives to a great extent from the ghetto: instruction is routinely given under the heading of catechesis to men and women who are to all intents and purposes pagan, and the sacraments of initiation and Christian marriage are celebrated as if the assumptions one could safely make of most Catholic families in the 1940s and 1950s still held true. There appears to be little analysis, at the level of pastoral policy and practice, of the massively changed situation. Instead there is a kind of cowardly permissiveness that avoids confronting unchristian, unrepentant dispositions and perpetuates the idea that sacraments are available to anyone, whether or not they appreciate their Christian significance. The Council certainly intended the Church to abandon many of the incidental features of Tridentine Catholicism, but only in order to rediscover the radicalism of the gospel. What seems to have actually happened is that we have become dispensers of cheap grace instead.

CHRISTIANITY'S PERPETUAL REVOLUTION

What is absent from this middle-class religion is the biblical concept of repentance and the conviction at the heart of the Christian faith that the authentic message of the gospel does not confirm and reinforce the bourgeois values of autonomy, property, stability, and success but disrupts them. The basic structure of Christian life, individually and communally, is: repentance, faith, discipleship. Christ began his own ministry by calling his hearers to conversion, the spiritual revolution by which men and women admit their guilt, turn away from sin, and surrender wholeheartedly to God (Mk 1:14-15). The early Church conducted its missionary work on the same basis, as Luke illustrates in the Acts of the Apostles. The apostles announced the message of salvation, and those who responded by believing came forward to be baptised as a sign of abandoning their old life, and began to take part in the new, radically different, life of the Christian community (Acts 2:37-41). The utopian picture of this life drawn by Luke in Acts 2:42-47 was not intended to be taken literally, but to show the high ideal of a communal existence inspired by Christian love (*agape*), and its distinctiveness in relation to the ordinary lifestyle of the pagan majority.

According to the Jesuit historian of liturgy, Josef Jungmann, the standards of the Christian Church were just as high about two hundred years later. Christians did not try to borrow propaganda techniques from the pagan world around them, or to dilute their message in the hope of broadening the Church's membership. In her efforts to attract converts, Jungmann wrote, the Church "maintained the stern standpoint of a decisive either/or. She did not want mere half Christians; she preferred to remain small in numbers rather than to be unfaithful to her principles, or endanger them." Catechumens were examined for the sincerity, honesty, and depth of their intention to follow Christ. They had to show, too, that their conduct corresponded with Christian ideals. There was no attempt at polite evasion or talk of receiving those in whom only a so-called "spark" of faith could be detected. The self-understanding of the Church in this period was that of the little flock, the leaven in the lump. Christians affirmed this identity in direct opposition to the larger pagan culture, which they saw, of course, as being afflicted by the blindness of unbelief.

Even after the conversion of Constantine, when Christianity won a new official status throughout the Roman Empire, pastors like Martin of Tours, Ambrose of Milan, Augustine of Hippo, and John Chrysostom had no doubts about the difference between the City of God and the earthly city, and resisted the trend towards assimilation with heathenism. One aspect of this, the vigorous defence of the Church's independence from interference by secular rulers, was the distinguishing mark of the Church in both the East and West during this time.

As Roman civilisation collapsed under the pressure of its own decadence and weakness, and of successive waves of barbarian invasion, every social and cultural value declined. Politicians were corrupt. The rich turned their backs on the poor and violent crime became more commonplace. Notions of justice and punishment grew more cruel and savage, dictated by the instinct for revenge and retaliation rather than any principle of fairness. Brutality, greed, lack of trust, sensuality, had a snowballing effect: the more people felt the structures of civilised society fall apart, the more they retreated into a mentality of personal survival and aggrandisement.

In the midst of this disintegration, many Christians

surrendered their faith and moral ideals, but a sufficient number of clear-sighted leaders in the Church maintained their faithful stewardship of the Christian mysteries and insisted on the principle (and on a continual movement) of reform – what Henri Daniel-Rops called the "perpetual revolution of Christianity." The best of the Christian communities lived out their faith in a God who was love, trust, compassion, respect, justice. Prophetic churchmen – bishops, ascetics, hermits, monks – denounced vehemently the exploitation of the poor by tribal princes and local barons. The Church founded schools and hospitals everywhere, while the cathedrals and monasteries fed and protected millions of homeless refugees and beggars. "During the most sombre period of the Dark Ages," Daniel-Rops wrote, "there appears the great idea which is to be fundamental through [the Church's] whole history, the idea of reform. Throughout the Middle Ages, whenever the truth of the evangelical spirit was in danger of being obliterated by infamy and mediocrity, there were always some men there to arise and remind Christians of the divine commandment: this is the task which is to be assumed in turn by the monks of Cluny in the tenth century, Pope Gregory VII in the eleventh, St Bernard in the twelfth, and Innocent III and the mendicant orders in the thirteenth."

History never repeats itself exactly, but there are significant points of comparison between the Dark Ages and our own. Like our predecessors of the fourth to the tenth centuries, we are also "Christians of the Twilight." The dominant mores in our own times are materialistic and sensual. Lack of moderation and an aggressive individualism has become the accepted norm of conduct. Appetite and egoistic will take precedence over conscience and innate moral sense. More importantly, these trends in thought and behaviour and moral attitude have infiltrated the Catholic community to almost exactly the same extent as the wider society. Many, especially the young, lack the critical and discerning ability that would enable them to distinguish what is compatible with Christian belief and what is not, and in the last analysis have the same outlook and values as persons of no religious faith at all.

If circumstances today are similar in some respects to those of the Dark Ages, the response of Church authorities in Britain is not. Besides the larger monastic movement – by which communities of dedicated men and women created centres of holiness, virtue and high intellectual culture – the Celtic world in the Dark Ages saw a period of missionary initiative, such as the Iona and Lindisfarne communities from which saints like Columba and Aidan evangelised whole regions without any of the advantages of transport or communication available to the Church today. Unlike their counterparts in that era, Church leaders since the Council have not followed a strategy of reform or "perpetual revolution" but of managerialism. The piecemeal updating and modernisation, which became fashionable after the Council, only disguised the fact that no radical renewal or structural change was going to be allowed. Fear of change, lack of imagination, and spiritual mediocrity has characterised the leadership of the period, not Christian boldness, intelligence and initiative. Bishops, in particular, have surrounded themselves with what amounts to a new class of advisors and committee apparatchniks whose main function is to protect their bosses from reality and stimulate a mood of comforting but illusory optimism. Documents, mission statements, and pastoral "visions" are launched by the various boards and commissions, oblivious of the fact that the huge majority of Catholics are now – in ecclesiocommitte jargon – "unchurched", and have no interest for such window-dressing, or any enthusiasm for renewal. There is a sort of institutional schizophrenia: behind the facade of modernisation and bureaucratisation, and the hectic schedules of meetings that now occupy the various levels of diocesan administration, the real situation is one of a pastoral and missionary policy-vacuum and a desperate clinging to the last vestiges of the ghetto.

It is totally characteristic of God that at certain strategic moments he demands that his people abandon their existing situation and venture forward on a journey into the unknown, with only their trust and faith in him as their security. This was Abraham's experience, and the experience of Moses and the Hebrew slaves of the Exodus. The Church's decline in these islands over the last thirty years, the numerous clergy scandals, even the destruction of the hopes of the immediate post-conciliar years, are an invitation to us to interpret what God is calling us to do, to repent, and to leave the comfortable homeland which has served us well for so long. Since the kingdom of God is not built by human effort but is received as grace from God, there is no need for an exhaustive, detailed blueprint for the future. But there are steps that could, and should, be taken to bring our pastoral plans and evangelising efforts into greater harmony with the gospel.

In any society or community the quality and integrity of the men and women in positions of leadership is crucial. The Church is no different. This has nothing to do with clericalism or an attitude that sees the priests or the hierarchy as alone important. But it means that those who lead have a profound responsibility. It is the clergy above all who have the task of announcing the Christian message, of interpreting the world in which the message is announced, as *Presbyterorum Ordinis* puts it, and of forming the Christian community in its fundamental attitudes (*PO* 4). In Luke's gospel Jesus speaks a terrible word to those who exercise this responsibility: "The servant who knows what his master wants, but has got nothing ready and done nothing in accord with those wishes, will be given a great many strokes of the lash" (Lk 12:47). We should not deceive ourselves or paint a false, rosy picture of current standards of Church leadership. Rather we should adopt the bold language of John's gospel: there are Christians, including many in high positions in the Church, who are not of the light but of darkness. They have not allowed the Good News of Christ to penetrate their hearts; they have not allowed themselves to be open to that deep change of vision and values, which is the essence of repentance and conversion.

EVANGELICAL SIMPLICITY

Before the Council, a certain austerity and asceticism was an accepted feature of priestly life. After the Council, this element of sacrifice was effectively abandoned. It was even seen by many as a sign of progress that the priest's way of life became more comfortable and secure, and closer to that of the middle-class whose needs he was being asked to service. Today, secular priests who live within the ordinary structures provided for them are not poor and their lifestyle is not one of evangelical simplicity. Their daily existence is free from financial worry and insecurity. They live very often in houses that are larger than most family homes, and employ staff to do domestic jobs that most people have to do for themselves. Their mental outlook and expectations regarding their standards of living – evinced, for example, by a fondness for expensive clothes, cars, and holidays – derive not from Christ's instructions to the apostles in this area (Cf. Lk 9:1-6) but from the values of the affluent, consumer society. This ensures that, contrary to God's will as revealed through the prophets and through the activities and preaching of his Son, clergy naturally identify with the interests of the comfortable and wealthy rather than those of the poor and marginal. And, of course, priests who lead a comfortable, anti-evangelical way of life are no challenge to middle-class congregations that are only too happy to spiritualise, and ignore, Jesus' teaching about money and possessions.

Any movements of clerical reform and missionary

renewal in the history of the Church – its monasteries, the canons regular of the Middle Ages, the congregations of the modern period like the Vincentians and the Redemptorists – have always included a radical simplification of priests' lifestyle as a means of closer imitation of Christ and, as such, as a means of greater missionary effectiveness. People know instinctively that indifference and detachment from material things is proof of faith in the kingdom which is not of this world (Jn 18:36). Conversely, worldliness is a sure sign of lack of faith, despite verbal affirmations to the contrary. "When you have a rich, well-fed priest," Abbé Pierre said in a lecture to the junior seminary at Rouen, "you can be sure that there will be whole pages of the gospel which he will never preach, because he can't." He went on, "A priest must love poverty, because it is only then that people will believe him when he says he loves God; for God is Love, and Love consists in sharing with those who suffer."

One contemporary Church leader who came to realise the truth of this was Archbishop Romero of San Salvador. Before he was killed he had already moved out of the grand episcopal palace where the bishops of San Salvador lived, and moved into a small flat in the grounds of a cancer hospice run by an order of nuns. When his cathedral was damaged very badly by an earthquake in 1978, Romero refused to have it repaired, because he thought it was immoral to spend money on maintaining Church property while so many men and women in his diocese lived in conditions of destitution. Actions and gestures such as these are a testimony of deep faith: nothing is to be sought except God's kingdom and its justice. In our country, among our leaders, this kind of faith is absent, and they are incapable of such detachment from buildings, worldly lifestyles, and purely human, local traditions.

The lives of innumerable saints show that faith, reform, and evangelical poverty have always gone hand in hand in the Church. It is only in our own time that we appear to think that we can renew our missionary capacities by bureaucratic rearrangements rather than by our willingness to convert and create within our communities a counterculture to the idolatrous and exploitative materialism of society at large. "Remain faultless and pure, unspoilt children of God surrounded by a deceitful and underhand brood, shining out among them like bright stars in the world, proffering it the Word of life" (Phil 2:15-16). The responsibility for this task, which is one of evangelization by example, lies primarily with the clergy. Spiritual leaders should lead.

TEAM WORK AND LAY PASTORAL MINISTRY

The deployment of available manpower, also, is frequently irrational. The burden of pastoral work in many places is unevenly and unfairly distributed among clergy. Side by side, in neighbouring parishes, some priests are virtually idle while others suffer nervous breakdown through overwork.

Especially in the smallest parishes, the tradition of providing the community with a resident priest should be broken. Instead of continuing to prop up a failing, antiquated model of parish life, priests should be organised in teams covering a wide pastoral area, centred on the largest parish, or in a geographically central location. Priests' workplace and living quarters should no longer be merged, as at present, so that they can establish a dividing line between work and free time and relaxation – not a selfish desire, but an essential condition for psychological and emotional well-being. Priests could continue to live apart from each other, if they wanted, but the entire pastoral workload for that area – hospital, school ministry, counselling, weddings, funerals in different churches, etc. – should be shared amongst the whole team. Since every Christian is called to be an evangelist, many areas of pastoral activity – catechesis, care of the sick, and others – should be carried out by teams of laymen and women who can easily be trained to the required level. This reflects the methods of the early Church, which did not concentrate all missionary and pastoral activity in the hands of the elders but spread the responsibility evenly throughout the entire community. If lay people are reluctant to take on these facets of the Church's life, then we should accept that, due to the community's lack of commitment, certain tasks will simply not be carried out and pastoral needs will be neglected.

For many years, lay people were schooled in a passive, almost infantile role. They were on the receiving end of the priest's "ministry", which consisted of a sort of professionalised Christian vocation. With dwindling numbers of ageing priests, this relationship now cannot continue, even if we wanted it to. Our parishes will have to become basic missionary communities as in the first centuries, or cease to exist. Unfortunately, the decline of the ghetto model of parish life is often lamented and resisted rather than taken as the opportunity for re-examination of what is important and a renewal of both attitudes and structures. There is a disproportionate pandering to conservative, traditionalist sentiment, and a desire not to offend, which only hampers the necessary reform. The members of the hierarchy in Britain for the most part regret the lack of vocations and their inability to staff every parish with priests, and only bring about changes reluctantly, when forced to by new circumstances, instead of pressing ahead now with new models of parish communities and the reformed clergy-lay relationships which would go along with them. In this area also there is need for repentance and faith, and greater willingness to confront petty, short-sighted, intransigent attitudes on the part of both the laity and the clergy.

The new forms of Catholic community will come, but we still have the choice of either directing events or of following them, responding – as has become our habit – with techniques of crisis management. The depressing truth is that, at present, the preference of Church leaders seems to be for the latter. As Adrian Hastings wrote, more than ten years ago: "Effectively, the only thing the faithful Catholic can do today is to ignore the hierarchy and its sinking ship, and try to get as many little lifeboats afloat – as many little basic communities – as possible. The massive decline of the institutional Catholic Church, at least in this country, is now irreversible. The survival of a vital tradition, however, if there are enough brave spirits about, is still possible."

TAKING UP THE CHALLENGE

Paul McDermott

Paul McDermott is a deacon who will be ordained priest later this year for the diocese of Westminster. He trained at the English College in Rome and at Allen Hall seminary in London. Prior to priestly formation, Paul obtained à degree in psychology from the University of Surrey and he has worked in health and service management in a major London hospital.

I am about to embark on a lifetime of saying Mass and hearing confessions; of anointing the sick and burying the dead; of marrying lovers and sleeping in an empty bed; of baptising babies and brooding over children I never had. It's a way of life that many people misunderstand: my parents think I'm a saint, my friends think I'm mad, and the world couldn't care less. Ahead of me is a lifetime of obedience to a bishop who might not remember my name, or bother to consult me about my appointment. A lifetime of praying the Office hour by hour, despite the ringing of the phone, the overrunning school-governors' meeting, and the midnight caller who has invented a great story as to why he needs the last pound in my pocket. Already the fears for my future begin to well up in me. How will I cope? Indeed if this litany of lament is all the priesthood is about then I shall stop writing now, give my breviaries to a fresh-faced first year, and leave. But there has to be more to it than this; it has to be deeper.

Priesthood is a mystery; and the challenge is to live out that mystery as best I can. The external functions and justified rows that make headlines on the clerical grapevine are only the dry skin of a mystery at the core of priesthood, the drama being acted out in the heart of the priest himself. My vocation itself is proof that I am in the realm of mystery. God has either been a very poor judge of character, or he is a compulsive gambler; he has taken risks with me that no one in their right mind would ever dare. But I am not alone: I only have to look around the Cathedral at the Chrism Mass to see the mystery of priesthood revealed. God calls the rich and the poor, the super-heroes and the villains, the straight and the gay, the black and the white, the conservative and the liberal, and me.

The most important challenge in being a priest is to try and be myself – the person that God has created and called – and to be ever open to the mystery of his will for me. This is no easy task because I'm entering into something that I will never totally understand or appreciate and I am doing so in a culture that sees priesthood as a scandal and a nonsense. The only way priesthood does make sense is when I slowly understand that I am called to live God's own mystery in my flesh and bones. This is an awesome vocation and it actually fills me with fear because it means taking risks on a God who I cannot see, and coming to trust that he knows what he's doing, even when I cannot fathom it out. The more I try to let go of my own self-dependence and trust in him, the more he will show me the purpose of it all.

The journey to priesthood for me has been primarily a discovery of who I am: the real me. And although this has been painful in parts I have come to realise, through this discovery, that being a priest is what gives meaning to my life; my way of holiness and salvation, my own winding road to God. So when I am asked why I want to be a priest, the only real answer I can give is that it makes utter sense to my life. Priesthood brings all of my experiences, joys and hopes together; and it can only do this because it is a mystery that is far greater than I am. The challenging thing now is to stay on that journey and to try and penetrate that mystery in the everyday life of my ministry.

As Catholics we are used to dealing with mysteries. I have fifteen of them, on a string of beads, in my pocket! But, because the concept is so popular, I think sometimes we are prevented from exploring its reality in depth. Perhaps a better term would be paradox. Recall what we believe in: one God and three persons; Jesus Christ, God and man; Christ present in Word and Sacrament; revelation guaranteed in Scripture and Tradition; a Church of hierarchy and laity; saints and sinners alike. It is this very Catholic "and" that gives the Church her dynamism and energy; it's the necessary tension which keeps us alive and open to change. And it is the paradoxical "and" in priesthood that animates the priest who is at once a person in his own right and in *persona Christi*, a sinner and an absolver of sins, a sexual person and a celibate. Yet in all of these "ands" it is the work of grace that prevents that tension from snapping and throwing us into crisis.

So the mystery is that Jesus has taken flesh in my heart, in my life, in my ministry, and principally in my weaknesses, as a priest. Priesthood is within me, not something exterior to my being. It is the life that God himself lives in my heart and in my veins. What I need to do is accept this precious gift of God; accept that he has called me to become his dwelling place, his altar and his sanctuary – where his drama of salvation continues to be played out. Because of this, when I pray the psalm, "So I gaze on you in the sanctuary," I gaze in awe at God in the sanctuary of my life and my experiences. He is present in my public persona, which often tempts me to lose touch with who I really am, and in the private heartache of loneliness and failure, which reminds me of my vulnerability and neediness. The mystery is within me, it is the very incarnation of Christ the Priest in my flesh and my bones. Such a gift has to be contemplated, reflected on and engaged with as it thirsts for my attention.

Since this mystery becomes our life, and holds within it our dynamism, passion and movement for growth, it can be quite disconcerting to meet priests who appear to be dried up, tired and angry. Such men seem to have become disconnected from the real stuff of their ministry – which isn't how to apply for money from the Lottery, or even particularly how to make Lent this year more meaningful, "especially for the under-fives." The stuff of priesthood lies in their own spiritual journey as priests, their own personal pilgrimage of life, which itself becomes a wellspring of salvation for the people they love and serve.

You may have heard all of this before and maybe you're as wary as I am with the trend to call all things that we don't understand a mystery. I agree, the word mystery has been thrown around too much. Even the secular world tells us that a spiritual awakening has begun in people, that they are looking for something more, for the transcendent, for a return to mystery. But the mystery that I am talking about is at its heart the Incarnation. It is the mystery not only of me, but of God-and-me; the God who has dared to enter my humanity, and so accompanies me as I try to live a human life as a human priest, among other human beings. That's the mysterious simplicity of it.

Yet this mystery is not an excuse for me to abandon the challenge of personal holiness. Indeed the temptation to disengage from the mystery of the Incarnation within me, to dilute its power in my life and conform myself to the world's values is always going to be a huge challenge because worldly power and promises are so exciting. Each time I go out into the Kings Road in London I pass by the people that I have always wanted to be, the people I could have become. Along just one mile, I rub shoulders with the rich and famous and find myself welling up with envy at the fast cars, the gorgeous faces, and the designer clothes – driven, kissed and worn by people of my own age and background. In just twenty minutes my heart is pulled apart as the world laughs in my face and I respond with the song

"It should've been me!" I know that a major struggle in my priesthood will be to maintain some inner harmony as the lure of money, sex and fame greets me everyday. The problem is that these values are so much part of me; I am so much a product of the culture that proclaims them. Without a commitment to the mystery of God's life in my tempted being, I can already picture myself buying into the fast car market and driving myself to destruction.

I think that the very real struggle to "be in the world but not of it" demands some sort of support for priests from within the Church which will help to galvanise and foster our own determination to become men of prayer and contemplation. Too often priests are forgotten: their needs are not met and they feel undervalued and overlooked. Certainly, without the paternal support of my bishop and the fraternal care of my fellow priests, the temptation to fall into isolation and hopelessness on one hand – or to jump into a hidden life among the "beautiful people" on the other – is hard to resist. If I am not supported as a man, as a celibate, and as a consecrated priest by the Church I love and the people I cherish, then the challenge to stay in ministry will be made even more difficult.

If it is true that I am ordained into the mystery of Christ, and that I undergo an ontological change, then the legitimate fears I have – my doubts about vocation, my fallings in love, my uncertainty about celibacy, and the ease of my temptation – take on a different light. Because my priesthood is not my own there is space enough to work to perfection, and not insist on perfectionism; my successes and failures can be my very means to holiness precisely because they are forgivable and utterly redeemable. And since the gift of this mystery is not for me alone, it gives me an exit from my worries about imperfection and personal failure as it demands that I give myself away to others. In other words, even my weaknesses and failure can be used to serve others. When people come to priests they want to encounter a fellow human being: body and soul, sinful and broken – but also one who has discovered a deep communion with the God who saves him. They don't come to a social worker, or a doctor of theology, or a psychologist; but to a man who knows God's love for him, intimately, painfully, and mysteriously. They come to meet Jesus himself. I wonder, when I become a priest: who will they meet when I open the door?

Thankfully such priests – such men who are themselves in the process of being redeemed as well as in the process of continuing Christ's work of redemption – are not hard to find. They don't all live in retreat centres and write best sellers. I am thinking here of the unsung heroes of our dioceses who have worked tirelessly for others often without any recognition from their peers or their superiors, even though their ministry has truly touched thousands of people and generations of the faithful and unfaithful alike. They are the priests who I instinctively think of going to see for some down-to-earth practical advice or for confession; priests who remind me that I am only human and not alone, because I can see in the man in front of me someone who has been through similar battles and has learnt to accept his humanity and let Christ redeem it. They are the ones who, behind the seemingly natural and mundane life of the parish, give a glimpse of the extraordinary and supernatural. The challenge for me is to try and be like them.

Many years ago Edward Schillebeeckx wrote a book called *Marriage: Human Reality and Saving Mystery*. Some of you may have read it all, or dipped into it. It is a book that traces the history of marriage and seems to have become a standard textbook for understanding the sacrament. I was struck mainly by its title. How suitable, with a minor adjustment, it would be as a title for the Mystery that I have been trying to talk about: *Priesthood: Human Reality and Saving Mystery*. What such a title means is that to be a priest is to be fundamentally a human being. Yet, as we know, if I want to be fully human I have to accept that it cannot happen without making a fundamental option for God in my life.

He reveals to me who I am, knowing me more than I know myself. When I say "yes" to God in baptism and particularly in the promises at ordination, I am basically saying "yes" to an intimate relationship with him, a living, growing and transformative partnership which is not a dream or an ideal but an essential part of my human reality. When I say "yes" to priesthood, I agree to the surrender and abandonment of my dreams and possibilities, my past and future, my sexuality and manhood, my natural urge to generate and procreate, into the unknown plan of God himself. I have to say "yes" everyday to God's own desire to live in me as God. But this is not a surrender to monotony or an abandonment of my liberty. It is based on an act of faith in a God who eternally wants me to be a priest, who desires my life to become his instrument of salvation, and who asks it of me out of love. Like the marriage contract, I hand over the blank cheque of my life, which I will honour regardless of the amount that God will fill in. I enter into a real, living partnership, a nuptial union between God and myself. But the question is do I want it? Like marriage, if I do not want this union with God then my commitment to the priesthood will be a shaky one. The problem is that many of us today do not know what we want. It seems the curse of modern culture that we have so many options available to us; that to choose to commit ourselves to one thing or another – even for a day, let alone a lifetime – is so difficult.

I recall the day I was accepted into the seminary. After trying my best to convince my bishop that I wanted to be a priest (and having rehearsed my reasons for most of the preceding week) I was struck by his closing remark. As I left his study, he said to me, "By the way, if ever you find that you don't want to be a priest, then get out!" I am sure that my bishop didn't mean that when I wake up and feel I can't face another Mass, or another dead baby, or another liturgy planning meeting, I should pack my bags and leave. What I think he meant was that my desires are important and that I cannot run away from them. Sordid as they may be sometimes, worrying as they often surely are, destabilising as they are prone to become, they are nevertheless the natural indicators of who I am and what I want as a man. So nowadays, when I am feeling low or confused, I look in the mirror and chant, "I am doing this because I want to do it." I actually believe that my deepest desires are also God's desires for me – with the proviso that he alone can and wants to satisfy them.

Dare I, then, contradict my bishop? I would suggest that when we least want to be a priest, perhaps then we should remain. Perhaps then the hour has come for us to discern again the mystery of Christ's priesthood in which we āre called to share. I say this because, if priesthood is Jesus' invitation to become his flesh and blood in our sophisticated third millennium, then we have to be prepared for that part of the mystery that is the simple way of the cross. The cross is the saving reality that strikes at the hole in my fragile human heart. I am reminded of it when I shed tears for others; when I feel I have been kicked in the teeth, rejected by the world and abandoned by friends and colleagues. Most of the time I can't bear to look at this void within me, it's too sensitive. Yet part of my vocation is to explore this black hole, to sit alone with it, accepting that it can somehow – must somehow – be the way to resurrection.

Many people think that seminary training is too long. But I think it should be as long as it takes for us start engaging with the cross in our lives, because it is the cross which will become our greatest gift for others. For many years I avoided such an idea; it was too painful even to imagine. But one day I said a prayer that changed my life. "Lord show me your cross in my life." Reflecting on it now, it was the most foolish thing I have ever done because the Lord heard my prayer and answered it. I was soon confronted with my own fragility and saw how I had been crucified by a certain absence of love, which for a long time had driven me into a cycle of despair, self-doubt and rejection. I learned the paradoxical beauty of powerlessness in the face of raging emotions and profound sorrow. Yet I believe that my vocation to priesthood comes from this experience of the cross. Although my own Calvary continues, it has become the very seedbed of my priesthood and I believe the wellspring of salvation for others. Priesthood in this sense has to be uncomfortable and painful, because it is a sharing in the priesthood of Christ – who is not only priest but also victim. The challenge lies in our choice of whether to follow Peter and run away, or to accompany John and stay at Golgotha, participating in some way in the horror and the mystery of the crucifixion.

Paul VI once said that what the world needs are not teachers, but authentic witnesses to the gospel. This means that as a priest I have to be a credible witness to the mystery of the incarnation in my life. I could quite easily teach the world the facts and figures of the gospel – that's what six years of lectures have helped me to do. But to be a witness is to be intimately engaged with the gospel in my own life. And, as we know, at the centre of this gospel is the experience of Crucified Love. Authentic priesthood is rooted in the once and for all, priestly act of Christ on the cross, where he is broken and poured out for the salvation of the world. If I dare to take up the challenge of priesthood today, I have to continue this work of Christ even to the point of my own breakdown and abandonment. Indeed I have not witnessed anything more moving and more priestly than seeing a man saying Mass who has suffered greatly either physically or mentally. When he says, "This is my body broken for you, my blood poured out for you," it is real, he means it. For me this is the model of priesthood that convinces me the most; this is the authentic witness of Christ's mystery in human flesh and blood. Until we allow the full horror and beauty of the cross to become a part of our lives, even if it is in secret, then I think we miss the point.

This all sounds rather dramatic – and some of you may well accuse me of suggesting that the authenticity of a priest is measured by the amount of times he falls, or by how much he pays a psychotherapist every week, or by how many admissions to a de-tox clinic he has made. Such ideas would indeed be rather fatuous. I am trying to highlight our need to be honest about where the Lord has planted his cross in our lives, because that holy place – our own personal Golgotha – will be the summit and source of our vocation and ministry as priests of the incarnation. Put quite simply, it's the place of our own transformation from death to new life; and the place where, if we humbly search, we will find God already present, loving us in our need, loving us into salvation.

If by becoming a priest I am called to live the mystery of the incarnation then at some point in my life, I have to accept myself as I as am; a man, human and fallen. But the saving reality is that I am transformed by grace, that Christ himself desires to take on my flesh and mortality, to live and minister through me, with me, and in me, for the salvation of the world. In my own life he reveals the Father's love for me, but with that comes the mission to pour out his love for others. Indeed, none of what I have said can remain my own property, it's all for others, for the people I serve, for the people who call me father.

Many say that the best priests are those who would have made great fathers. This may be true and can be yet another reason why so many of us melt inside when we see our brothers or our best friends with their children. We are confronted with the picture of what some of us would have been like if we had not got ordained. We see the joy that being a father brings and we secretly fantasise whether perhaps we would be just as good – or even better – dads than they. Even though I will not become a biological father, I would hope that my fatherhood as a priest will still tap into the gifts and skills that would have made me a good dad. Even though I am celibate, I don't have to be frigid. My sexuality and my capacity for love are still God's gift and his command to use them remains even after I commit myself to life-long celibacy. When I hide or ignore this life-giving side of myself, and when I convince myself that I don't long to give and receive love, then very quickly human reality hits home and I have to choose what to do with the energy that such longing begets. All around our dioceses we have reminders of this human need to generate: in the parish centres, churches, schools and pastoral projects which priests of old have built almost single-handedly. So I am confronted with the unavoidable question of how I can use my natural need and desire to procreate appropriately and leave my mark as a testimony to my existence. Too readily I can settle for frustration and fall into despair, rather than accepting that I can do something productive and healthy with my energy. It doesn't have to be sexual but it does have to be directed by love.

In recent years it has become the trend to have ordination booklets that give a running commentary on what is going on, what the symbols mean and who the readers are. These are very useful not just for the bishop, but also for strangers to Church and for the coach load of agnostics that we tend to invite. What moves me most, though, is the cue-change after the prayer of ordination which sums up what the whole ceremony is about. It usually says something like, "Now Fr X gets up and kisses his mum." In just one sentence we are simply told that X is now a father, that he has changed. That for me is the challenge of priesthood in a nutshell. To become a good and faithful father. How do we become good fathers? After all, society is in crisis about both the function and desirability of fatherhood and what it is to be a man. Where do we look for a model of fatherhood, when perhaps our own fathers have left little to be desired and our spiritual fathers have not shown us the love that a son deserves? I think we have to turn again to the mystery to which, through ordination, we are configured: the mystery that is the person of Christ, the Son of the Father, who has chosen to become indelibly a part of our nature. In Jesus we see the Father, in Jesus we do the will of the Father, in Jesus we reveal the Father to an orphaned world. As a priest, how

I do this, where I do this, when I do this and what I wear to do this, really does not matter. As long as I try to do it, and take the mystery of the incarnation in my life as both the beginning and end of my ministry, then I can be confident that the challenges of priesthood will not overwhelm me.

MINISTERING TO THE MINISTERS

Michael Griffin

A priest of the diocese of East Anglia, Michael Griffin has been ordained for twenty-seven years and has worked in a number of parishes throughout East Anglia and North-amptonshire. Until recently he was the parish priest of St Laurence's in Cambridge. Currently he is engaged in supply work throughout the diocese, allowing other priests to take sabbaticals and extended retreats from their parishes. He has also been involved in a pilot scheme of clergy appraisal which has been operating within his diocese.

Despite the fact that most clergy of my acquaintance loathe them, I find myself fascinated by Frs. Ted Crilly, Dougal McGuire and Jack Hackett, marooned as prisoners on Craggy Island. The stars of Channel 4's "Father Ted" are quite unlike any clergy you will ever meet, but certain features of their caricatures are compelling and I wonder where I have met them. The answer is, of course, in the mirror. They may represent only a tiny bit of the truth, only a sliver of the whole picture of the priesthood – but what a sliver. In Dougal I see myself newly-ordained: wet behind the ears and utterly clueless; emerging from years of seminary for-mation, for what? In Ted I see myself having discovered that the real formation I should have been given was simple and practical: bars and licences, tours and pilgrimages, raffles and fund raising – the real stuff of parish life; middle management ducking and weaving. In Jack there is the spectre of that brokenness and bitterness too long repressed. His agony at finding himself for one moment sober and still on that **** island sends him back to the bottle and oblivion. They share a common life and there is a sexist subculture with Mrs Doyle who answers the door and makes the tea. Diocesan support is in the form of Bishop Len, who has exiled each of them to Craggy Island as punishment. Appraisal is delivered according to the episcopal model in short sharp bites. Affirmation is not on his agenda. Been there, done that, bought the tee shirt.

Like all genuine humour this picture of the lives of Catholic priests contains a grain of truth. Twenty-five years ago, life in many presbyteries would have had similarities with the parochial house on Craggy Island. Now such a place is a rarity. For all its faults the old system did provide support and protection of a kind for the priest: a degree of common life, sensible and regular food, conversation of sorts. At its best it worked well. My own early experience of parish life was in an inner city presbytery with a number of priests with very different approaches. It was an encouraging and stimulating time. Nowadays, if priests happen to share a house, there is a different expectation. No common life, separate television sets, even separate fridges – probably quite separate prayer life. At least there remains the possibility of conversation and companionship. It raises lots of issues. How should we be trained? What exactly is our job? How should we support one another? How should the structures support us? What happens when we crumble? What will happen when we get old? And in the meantime, how do we keep faith with God and with the Church?

In the twenty-seven years since my ordination as a diocesan priest much has changed in the world at large. The climate of fear comes no longer from the external threat of the bomb, but seems now to be a sinister internal one – the destruction of the planet by our collective greed, exploitation and apathy. In the Church, too, many things have changed. The direction of change is sometimes the reverse of what we had hoped for. Ministry in the Church is still largely the preserve of celibate males. Many things which did appear to change for a while have reverted to their former state. The autonomy of local conferences of bishops has been severely curtailed with the new centralisation of authority in the Church. We seem to be witnessing a creeping infallibility, not of the Magisterium, but of the civil service, the Roman Curia. The institutional face of the Church, from my point of view, is now quite different. After the Council there was a strongly felt sense of the prophetic nature of the Church. There was a renewed and noble simplicity about its humble invitation to dialogue with all people and systems. Its constant urging of justice on behalf of the poor, and its efforts for peace, were made all the more effective by the understated and seemingly vulnerable and anguished figure of the Pope. The modern Church by comparison seems to have found its old triumphal clothes in the wardrobe and decided to give them a new airing. The public face of the Church is undoubtedly more self-confident and cuts a more powerful figure on the world stage. Because of this it is not easy to see just how the priest of today is a counter cultural symbol. A newly confident clerical culture that has reduced the Scriptures and the conciliar documents to footnotes in the Catechism and the Code of Canon Law may be the desired ideal for some. For others the signs of the times seem to call for something different. Weakness, poverty, silence and celibacy all give witness to the rumour of God. They may be the necessary means of martyrdom in our age.

The newly ordained priests of today have been through a selection process and a more coherent formation than have priests of my generation. They come from very different backgrounds which reflect the changes in the rest of society. They emerge from seminary better equipped pastorally. Often they have a very definite idea of what a priest is and what he is for. A crisis of identity is no longer fashionable. In many areas of the world the Church is growing rapidly. Vibrant communities and full seminaries. In terms of success at the numbers game all is well. In Europe the picture is one of decline. Population shifts and cultural changes have left church buildings redundant, clergy as a dying breed and the people largely indifferent to things religious. At least this is what I read in the papers. Happily it is not my experience. Parish communities thrive, and people still come to Mass – perhaps with greater freedom and commitment than before. The majority of priests live out their calling faithfully and joyfully. Despite the best efforts of the clergy to quench the Spirit of God renewing the Church we have not succeeded! I live in a part of the country (UK) which is experiencing rapid growth. We do not have any redundant churches as yet, and with the influx of a large number of former Anglican clergy, we have an "elegant sufficiency" of clergy (in terms of filling gaps on the diocesan schedule). We can keep the show on the road for the time being. Whether it is the right show on the right road is another question.

FAITH

Against this background the crises and problems that affect priests come from many sources. Perhaps the least discussed is that of faith. The population at large has abandoned organised religion, and settled on any passing fad to fill the gap. The human spiritual hunger is now filled from any one of a large number of sources. The bookshelves in bookstores now put together aromatherapy and white witchcraft along with the Scriptures and more traditional spiritual reading. It is often said that many people throughout the world are sacramentalised but not evangelised. I wonder, is it possible for us priests to be theologised but not evangelised? The clergy are suspicious of many forms of renewal. We complain of too much enthusiasm and lack of balance. Yet if we are not continually renewed we may find that we have settled for a gospel of our own making. The task of setting up effective means of support for the clergy includes an attempt to engage us in a lifelong process of renewal and growth in our understanding of the mystery of God.

The pattern of ministry changes throughout history according to how each age understands the Church, the Trinity and the incarnation. "Saving souls" was the ministerial model for an ecclesiology that saw the Church as an island of grace in a sea of sin. Perhaps one of the great rediscoveries of our present age has to do with recapturing a sacramental vision: that all of creation is graced and is loved into being by God, who is nothing other than perfect self-giving love. God loves creation into being – God loves me, therefore I am. A minister's task is to bring to the world the news of what already is, namely, that all of creation is loved and saved by God. Not as a result of our efforts at conversion, but simply as a result of who God is. Helping people to celebrate and articulate that is difficult. The Church is the sign of the mysterious presence of God. The priest needs to work harder than before to be a servant of the mystery. The more the institutional Church apes the civil powers with words and deeds of control and denunciation, the more it obscures the fragile treasure in its charge. I wonder how many people have in fact embraced from our preaching a notion of a God 'out there' who is as eager as any Roman Dicastery to spot and punish any deviation from the norm? Belief in such a God is, of course, the constant temptation that the first commandment warns us against. This is the kind of God against whom most of the parables of Jesus are aimed. Belief in such a monster cripples us for life and brings the gospel into disrepute.

What you believe about God shapes the way you pray. The public prayer of the Church through sacramental activity can easily become just another task for the priest. I wonder if our intellectual training really helped us to be pray-ers, or do many of us just think thoughts about God when we pray? There is a basic 'sacred technology', which is concerned with how to pray with the mind, and the heart, and also with that other inner centre where the God of the present moment is experienced. It may be that this was taught at seminary and I failed to notice or learn. Or it may be that it was taken for granted that we knew. The daily review of life or *examen* is a well-tested means of self-supervision.

STRESS

Other problems for the clergy have to do with the sources of stress. Most people today are aware of stress as part of life. Stress is of course necessary to healthy functioning. There are a number of stressors in the lives of priests that need to be monitored. I was trained to live in community but have spent twenty-three years out of twenty-seven living alone. Community life, of course, presents a great opportunity for mortification, but the perils of living alone are more subtle. The solitary life can accentuate eccentricities and quirks, it can make you immensely selfish. It is easy to become the centre of one's own universe and to see life as just a film in which I am the principal star. Loneliness can be an unrecognised or unacknowledged companion. Acquiring a dog is the best remedy on the market. Compensations for the stresses in the lives of celibate clergy have traditionally been seen as money, sex and power. This is the stuff of newspaper headlines. It is also the stuff of the New Testament warning concerning the spiritual battle against the world, the flesh and the devil. Alcohol dependency, depression and suicide are said to affect the lives of many in the medical profession and probably other professions also. The clergy have a low suicide rate, but share in the common problem of alcohol abuse and depression. Perhaps some reasons for stress and burnout among the clergy are the following:

• The increasing and unrealistic demands and expectations from the "consumer".

- One priest living alone doing the work which two or three did twenty-five years ago.
- Increasing bureaucracy, form filling and work concerning the governing of schools.
- The public image of the priest following the recent cases involving the sexual abuse of children.

I remember noting from the late 1980s the steadily mounting pressure from the rising number of people calling at the presbytery door. No longer just passing tramps in need of tea and a few bob, but the homeless and hopeless, the victims of that government policy called care in the community (strictly limited to Monday to Friday, 9am-5pm). There were few resources or little time to do much except offer sympathy. The growing feelings of guilt were fuelled by the constant and indiscriminate needs of parishioners. "Father, did you know there are no loo rolls in the parish room? What are you going to do about it?" "Where are the keys to the hall/shed/church/school?" "Can you give me the fare to Aberdeen?" "Why is my Mass intention not on the list?" A sense of being trapped, where the trivial and important merge, where there is no time to give to those in genuine need, and certainly no time to give anything to yourself.

This is not a problem that can be solved by collaborative ministry, since that seems actually to increase rather than to diminish the priest's involvement in things. It is difficult to legislate for all this. Certainly a "hardening of the ought-eries" is useless. I find it hard to believe that the present system requiring the priest to live on site, over the shop and out of the till, makes for good psychological health. Fr Michael Hollings was inspirational to me and many others of my generation. It took me too long to realise that the 'open house' system, which he advocated and practised so successfully, is a great idea if you live in a big city and have quite a staff on hand to make it happen. It is quite a different thing when you are not a saint, and live alone, and find yourself quickly swamped. There are, of course, priests who manage to make the presbytery into a home with a warm and welcoming atmosphere. There are many others who live in buildings where each room feels like an office and where there is no personal sign of a flesh and blood human being on the premises. "No word that he has not lived in vain. No word that he laughed or wept or loved or lived" (Emerson). Perhaps total availability belongs to the past when there were more clergy, and we should now try to make it possible for clergy to "go home" without developing a nine to five mentality. The business of having a home, or some means of "getting a life" brings up the question of warm and cold sins. The warm sins are the familiar ones – sins of passion. Perhaps the more deadly are the cold sins: those arising "not from an excess of passion but from a fear of passion. The product of a calculated apathy, sustained only by the embers of a dying soul." Coldness, and the fear of human relationships and intimacy; spiritual boredom, the fear of failure and inadequacy; meanness; lack of self-knowledge and self-awareness; "brains on stilts" – in other words, a disembodied spirituality or theology: all these are the cold sins.

Some English speaking countries seem to have in place very professional systems of support for their clergy. Personnel boards who deal with appointments and retirements. Financial departments with a proper system of pension and retirement provision and health care. Accommodation away from the Church premises and a salary system without the inequalities of our own. While all these things need serious attention, there is a danger of over emphasising the managerial culture. Our own slightly haphazard system has many dangers, and is open to exploitation, but does preserve some simple gospel values of poverty and availability and service. Perhaps we need to identify more clearly what we value about our present lifestyle.

Diocesan priests are theologically dependent on their bishop to give meaning to their ministry. I have found that the relationship with the bishop is a make or break matter in my life as a priest. The diocese is simply a collection of parishes (and not, as some would like to say, an administrative subdivision of the Church of Rome). The local Church is a combination of communities under the care of a bishop, who is the visible sign of unity and communion. The parish as a theological entity needs to be given a higher profile. It is the place where the majority of Catholics first hear and experience the gospel. The job of the parish priest has often been seen in the past as second-class. The successful career priest moves away from the coal face of parish life as soon as he can into the area of academia or bureaucracy. Only those with no ambition or talent are left to tend the grapes in the vineyard. There is an assumption that anyone who is ordained can run a parish. Bishops rely heavily on people who have left religious communities with their own spirituality and charism to keep up the diocesan manpower. If anyone can do it then it begins to matter less who does it. Anyone is suitable to go anywhere. This often shows up in the manner in which moves take place. Twice in my life I have been moved by answer-phone. To leave parish A on Monday and begin at parish B on Friday is simply unacceptable. It speaks volumes about the underlying theological and psychological assumptions. It says first of all that parish communities don't matter. They should be glad to have anyone to come and say Mass for them. It says also that priests don't matter as individuals. Any horse will run on any course. It also makes the movement of clergy an instrument of punishment. The bishop moves you if he has too many complaints; or the bishop moves you if he thinks you are becoming too cosy; or – more usually – the bishop just moves you because you have become part of a chain which starts with Fr Awkward getting his own way in Nether Wallop. Because I am not a bishop I can say that this is a poor state of affairs. I am sure that as a bishop the appointment of clergy is a great headache and a difficult task. Any improvement in the situation, however, should not depend on whether the bishop is Mr Nice or Mr Nasty. If a bishop is too busy then he should appoint others to have the pastoral care of the clergy as their main responsibility. It should be possible for individuals to express a desire to move or to stay as part of an ongoing review and appraisal of their state of life. There should be a structure that allows the movement of personnel to be an adult choice. On the other hand – and equally importantly – a parish has the right to some kind of continuity of ministry. To subject a parish to a new approach without considering its history is to treat it without seriousness. To allow a priest to spend thirty years at the same address despite the needs of the parish for growth is to do the same. The system whereby religious appoint superiors for a term (once renewable) seems to have much to commend it.

First appointments form attitudes that last. I think the days are gone when priests were sent to the traditional curate breaker simply because someone had to go. My first appointment as a priest was to a highly innovative and encouraging setting where there was a steep and enjoyable learning curve. Attitudes to so many things are picked up without noticing. Sexism, clericalism, defeatism, and so on. I have seen many priests take several years to recover from an initial discouraging appointment. I wonder also if some kind of orientation course would be beneficial for those moving into their first appointment as parish priest. Also there is a need for an extended period between appointments, almost a grieving period. A time to let go of some issues and to take a fresh look at a new challenge.

The task of supporting ministers must begin in seminary as a task which will continue for life. If this is not the case then all schemes of support will be seen as remedies for the weak. Something that is optional quickly becomes redundant. The notion that every minister needs a minister should be built into the priest's psyche. What other profession would throw its expensively trained practitioners into the field without ever requiring them to read a book, update their knowledge and skills, be accountable to anyone, or simply take care of themselves as we do? It is too late to take a sabbatical when breakdown threatens. It is too late to seek spiritual direction when the dark night is the only channel available. It is too little too late to treat all forms of clergy distress from alcoholism to sexual dysfunction as qualifications for entry to a religious sanatorium. The priest exercises a role as counsellor. Presumably there is now provision for this training in seminaries. A basic assumption of the counselling process for the therapist is that the counsellor needs also to be a client. Individual therapy is a prerequisite for those engaged in skilled helping with another person. Such an idea must be built into the training a priest receives. He must take for granted that he will always be in need both of professional supervision and personal therapy. Only then will the kind of resistance one sees among the clergy to anything beginning with "psych-" be overcome.

Training to be a skilled listener is hard work and should not rely on natural charm. The ability to "convert life into truth", which some say is the preacher's task, can only happen if there is some way for the priest to reflect on his life and to develop the ability to discern the movement of the Spirit in his particular life and setting. This process goes hand in hand with the business of appraisal. There are those who are horrified by the idea of clergy appraisal. Some say it trespasses on the territory of the spiritual director, or that it could become an oppressive weapon in the hands of unscrupulous superiors. I see it as something altogether simple and necessary. Priests need feedback and they don't get it. "Lovely sermon, Father" may flatter the ego temporarily, but usually is of little value – and neither is "Absolute rubbish, Father." I think that priests need feedback from significant sources. In many ways we need those in the know to acknowledge what we do, and the struggles that we face, and to say "thank you" – or even "no thank you." I realise that this argues for an appraisal model to be adopted where the bishop is the appraiser, and that this would put an impossible strain on most bishops. Perhaps we must settle for a model that includes a mixture of appraisers.

The commonest form of feedback in the world is from friends. I believe this to be a very delicate area for us. We may have bolt holes if we are lucky. We often impose ourselves on families who are kind enough to adopt us. But there are priests who seem either not to need or to have friends. An American bishop is on record as saying that when a priest leaves the ministry he always asks him "Do you have any priest friends?" and the answer is invariably, "No." We make friends in seminary and may imagine that the friendship persists, but often the years slip by and our friends have become no more than acquaintances. There are of course obvious dangers here for us, but perhaps the biggest danger of all is to fall victim to the cold sin of having no friends at all.

This has an impact on our continuing spiritual formation. Some priests seem very successful in finding and keeping a spiritual director. My own experience has been patchy. I find there is a need to hear the words of absolution which, alas, I do infrequently. There is also a different need to try to articulate something of the general direction of my life. There is a need to moan, to let off steam, or just to try to be me. Maybe no one soul friend can do all these things. If I do not articulate the experiences of day-to-day life with another person I cannot discern what God might be up to with me. The temptation to rugged individuality and to go it alone is perhaps the hallmark of the diocesan priest. I have received much encouragement in the past through the Ministry to Priests programme, and also through the Jesus Caritas fraternity. In some dioceses these or other similar groups seem to flourish. Elsewhere the groups seem to lose their initial energy and settle down to be a minority interest. Perhaps the support structures will constantly change their shape. What must not change is the acknowledged need for support structures for those in ministry. Whatever final form they take, such structures would clearly be of benefit if they were to include the following:

- A clear job description, which can be the basis of review and continuing appraisal.
- A sabbatical requirement to be built into the diocesan plan.
- Continuing education and lifelong learning for the minister to be promoted as essential for ministering to others.
- The appointment of an episcopal vicar for clergy (with or without the title), whose job is the pastoral care of the clergy.
- A national plan for the financial nuts and bolts of clergy remuneration and pension provision.

Either the pattern of ministry must radically change beyond the celibate male model, which seems increasingly un-likely, or else we must take steps to invest in the ministers we have.

EPILOGUE

Another book on priesthood? This was my initial reaction when ST PAUL'S Publishing asked me to produce this work. It was the reaction, too, of a number of my contributors. What else can be written to add to the already existent hundreds of thousands of words in print from people like Basil Hume, Michael Hollings, Michael Ramsey, Tony Philpot and their ilk? Interestingly it was Tony Philpot, the author of *Brothers in Christ* and *Priesthood in Reality* (and a fellow priest of my own diocese), who was most encouraging and supportive. "I wish more pastoral priests would write," he said to me when we discussed the project. Having spent the past year struggling with this book and with the demands of parochial ministry, I can understand why they don't. It hasn't been an easy task by any means; but it has been immensely fruitful. The pleasure (and toil) of editing the chapters from my contributors leads me to agree with Tony's conclusion. I wish more priests would write. At the very least, I wish more would share in some way with their people (and with their brother priests) their own stories. Their lives and the theology by which they live their lives are undoubtedly worth being told again and again. Our theology of priesthood must never be allowed to become merely a clinical exercise, or a purely academic pursuit. It will always be much the richer for its drawing upon the pastoral practice of everyday priests.

As I write these last few words, I am reminded that today is Low Sunday and that the Gospel we have just celebrated is the story of Doubting Thomas (Jn 20:19-31). It is a familiar pericope. Thomas misses out on the initial encounter with the Risen Lord and refuses to believe his confreres unless and until he can touch the very wounds with which the crucifixion had scarred his Lord. A week later he gets his wish. "Here, Thomas," says the Risen Christ, "put your finger here; look, here are my hands. Give me your hand; put it into my side. Doubt no longer but believe." Thomas has to feel and touch the Crucified One before he can accept the Risen One. He has to look upon the marks of suffering and death before he is able to see and accept the Eternal Life that stands before him. It is a common theme that seems to come out of the writings in this book: the theme of conversion, of challenge, of facing the cross.

An image of vocation that I often use in prayer is the image of a jigsaw. Slowly, and bit by bit, as I endeavour to follow the Lord and answer his call, I am piecing together my life and beginning to see what I am meant to be. As I respond more deeply to God, so another part of the jigsaw slots into place and I am gradually re-created, being made ready for the glory of that new creation promised by the Risen Christ himself. Recently – perhaps, to be honest, only in the writing and editing of this book – I have begun to realise that a sizeable piece of my jigsaw which has been missing for quite some time is actually (and rather frighteningly) cross-shaped. Now I feel a little like Thomas. I stand before my Lord and feel myself invited to touch his hands and his side; to feel his wounds; to accept his cross in my own life and priesthood. However much I shy away from such a vocation – and believe me, I do – I know that as it was for the doubting twin, so it will be for me. Unless and until I accept that painful invitation, I shall never move on to a deeper faith or to a more authentic exercise of priestly ministry. Only in embracing the wounds of crucifixion shall I finally be made ready to be embraced in the arms of resurrection.